Virtues for Ordinary Christians

The **CHURCH** book series from Sheed & Ward focuses on developing discipleship and leadership, fostering faith formation, and moral decision-making, and enhancing the Church's worship and social ministry. Titles in the series address clergy, laity, and religious on topics and issues that concern the whole people of God.

Series Editor: Karen Sue Smith

Virtues for Ordinary Christians

James F. Keenan, S.J.

SHEED & WARD
Franklin, Wisconsin

As an apostolate of the Priests of the Sacred Heart, a Catholic religious order, the mission of Sheed & Ward is to publish books of contemporary impact and enduring merit in Catholic Christian thought and action. The books published, however, reflect the opinions of their authors and are not meant to represent the official position of the Priests of the Sacred Heart.

1999

Sheed & Ward
7373 South Lovers Lane Road
Franklin, Wisconsin 53132
1-800-558-0580

Printed in the United States of America

Library of Congress Cataloging-in-Publication Data
Keenan, James F.
Virtues for ordinary Christians / by James F. Keenan
p. cm.
ISBN 1-55612-908-4 (alk. paper)
1. Virtues 2. Christian ethics—Catholic authors.
I. Title.
BV4630.K44 1996
241'.4—dc21

95-46594
CIP

2 3 4 5 / 02 01 00 99

Contents

For

Sean

✵

Acknowledgments

THIS WORK WAS NOT DONE ALONE. WHEN I FIRST STARTED writing for *Church* I regularly sent my drafts to three people who gave me very helpful comments: Patricia Beattie Jung, Marilyn Martone, and Alex Manly. Alex's wonderful parish at Saint Joseph's in Kings Park, Long Island was also a source for many ideas on these pages. At *Church*, Karen Smith was extremely supportive, as were Phil Murnion and the rest of the National Pastoral Life Center. Likewise, my community at 10 Martin Street listened to me and engaged me considerably, especially Brian Daley and John O'Malley. In writing these new essays, Marty Calkins has provided all sorts of background commentary on virtue, while Cathy Kaveny and Liz Schorske have given me insights into humor.

I wrote the new ones at Princeton. Being here was made possible by a fellowship provided by the Center of Theological Inquiry. For this I want to thank Dan Hardy, Bill Lazareth, and Wallace Allston and the benefactors of the CTI. At Princeton I received great personal support particularly from John Coleman, the community at the Aquinas Institute and the wonderful staff at CTI: Maureen Montgomery, Linda Sheldon, Kate Le Van, and Mary Beth Lewis.

Other than Robert Heyer and others at Sheed & Ward only one person has read the entire manuscript. Thus I thank Sara Wuthnow for her comments, especially those that coaxed me away from idealism. Finally, this book is a collection not of essays but of narratives. Many of them deal with my family. It seems only right that I should dedicate it to one member and so to Sean, my brother, who has taught me about love, fidelity and humor, here's something in return.

✵

Introduction

ONE DAY I GOT A CALL FROM MICHAEL WALSH WHO SERVED on the Committee on Doctrine at the National Conference of Catholic Bishops. He was phoning for some friends in New York and he wanted to know what I thought of a short list of moral theologians who were being considered to author the morals column at *Church.* I thought it was an impressive list; while hanging up, I said, "Mike, if they all say no; I'll take it; I'd love to do a column on virtue." A few weeks later I got the column.

I wanted the column because I wanted a place to work out my ideas about virtue and ordinary adult life. I wanted to address not curious Christians, but thinking ones. I wanted to communicate with somebody interested not in whatever contemporary topic was dividing the Church, but rather in what could be foundational for our family and community lives. I wanted to find common ground. Moreover, rather than looking to principles or rules that govern some particular and specific complex actions, I wanted to look at ordinary life. To do that, I turned to the virtues.

In theology today, there is a constant criticism that the virtues are soft, inexact, and lofty. Against that challenge I wanted to present them as concrete, practical, useful and necessary. I did not see the virtues as ideas, but as practices. Thus I turned to familiar stories and tried to weave into these narratives something from the fabric of our tradition.

Over the years a variety of hard-working, thinking, practical-minded people have told me that they read my column. It's for them that I do these essays. It's for you that I have put together this collection with eight new essays. Together they capture my view of how to grow as an ordinary Christian. I hope they speak to you.

Part I

An Introduction to Virtue

ONE

The Habits of Being

NINE YEARS AGO I QUIT CIGARETTE SMOKING. FOR THE FIRST eighteen months I was fine, but while doing doctoral studies in Rome my resolve faltered. Before long I was smoking again, this time with a large percentage of the Roman population for whom smoking is not as vicious a habit as it is in Boston.

Five years ago I returned from Rome determined, among other things, to quit smoking. I planned this fairly carefully. I prepared myself for the fact that I would probably gain an unavoidable ten pounds and that I just had to accept it. (I could lose it later, I opined.) I decided to tell everyone I knew I was quitting. (I reasoned that in the event of temptation, my health might not provide sufficient resolve; I knew that shame and embarrassment would.) Finally, since I smoked obsessively whenever I wrote, I planned to do no writing at all for the first month.

I quit smoking on Ash Wednesday. I took all my clothes to the cleaners . . . ventilated my room . . . threw out ashtrays. I rewarded myself with movies and ice cream for the first week. I went to no parties. I jogged a lot. And I stayed away from a few doubting friends who were convinced I couldn't do it. On occasion I still have a dream that I smoke, but in reality I don't. I also don't know what to do about the ten pounds I gained.

Because the moral life is concerned with ordinary life, morality cannot be reserved to a few actions of great significance. Every human act is a moral act. The way we talk, the time we spend, the plans we make, the relationships we develop all constitute the moral life. Morals is not primarily the study of grave actions; rather it is the study of human living. And being human is as complicated and frustrating as finding the right moment to quit cigarettes.

Developing Moral Practices

Ordinary human life is complicated because the variety of relationships, tasks, and personalities that constitute humanity intersect. In order to handle these complexities, we develop "practices." In his famous book, *After Virtue,* Alasdair MacIntyre argues that a practice is regular activity that shapes us in such a way that we develop dispositions to act in particular ways. Practices form habits. For instance, to deal with the stress of having to write or to meet people I got into the practice of smoking. Unfortunately, the practice of smoking at my desk and at parties extended to the habit of smoking everywhere else. Practices form us.

In order to deal with life's demands we adopt certain practices. Consider driving. We react to the presence of other cars on the road in various ways. Some drivers develop the practice of tailgating. Others stay at a steady thirty mph in the passing lane. Some practice the art of passing, while others look for the perfect car to follow at a few car lengths. Along with these practices, we each have our preferred lanes as well. And we each figure at what speed we should drive: above, at, or under the legal speed limit. These practices become habits. Sometimes the practices we develop on the road appear as habits at social gatherings: the passers, followers, tailgaters, and passive aggressives are not only found on the expressway.

We are continuously adopting practices to handle such simple activities as waking up, eating breakfast, showering, going to work, writing letters, making calls, greeting friends, playing sports, entertaining, driving, doing laundry, preparing meals, taking notes, using the computer, wearing clothes, dining, going to bed, reading, meeting new people, walking through shopping malls, relating to parents and children, listening, watching TV and brushing our teeth. These regular practices become habits, which in turn become deeply ingrained in and constitute particular dimensions of our lives.

These habits make us who we are. But as MacIntyre is more inclined to argue, certain practices engage us more profoundly than others. Two of these practices concern states of life and occupation.

State of Life and Occupation

About the first, for instance, I am a religious, living in community. Although there are some analogies to family life (in my community we cook, shop, clean and do the laundry; we watch TV together, have cookouts, and welcome one another's guests as our own), there are fundamental differences between the two. When it comes to flexibility, give and take, getting over arguments, appreciating differing personalities, and handling emergencies, my sister and brother-in-law are far more adept after fifteen years of marriage with two talented and active children than I am after twenty-two years of religious life. The privacy and independence that religious or clerical life requires are foreign to the responsibilities of family life. These state-of-life practices form the most profound habits in each of us.

Our work, too, constitutes formative practices. For example, before being a state investigator, my Dad was a New York City police officer for twenty years. That "practice" had its own language (I grew up thinking that all men told stories about "perpetrators") and its own hierarchy of values (he believed in responsibility, standards, punishment, availability, and courage). The "force" had its stories, and he told them as concretely and specifically as he lived them. On Manhattan South Homicide Squad, he came into contact regularly with people who literally used others. He despised these pushers and pimps, but developed a profound respect for drug addicts and prostitutes; he saw regularly that though they fought (usually unsuccessfully) for dignity and survival, they still managed to think of and protect their neighbor. As a result my Dad habitually walked away from hypocrites and anyone else who exaggerated their condition. He loved integrity and hated liars. Likewise his practice of investigating several "suspects," before making a "determination" made him a man slow to judge. Once he made his decision, however, he did not change his mind easily. He was not a teacher, doctor, nurse, priest, or sanitation engineer, he was a cop: twenty years of that practice made him one.

Lasting Changes Take Time

When we think of the moral life we sometimes forget just how deep our habits are and just how long it took to form them. Instead we get rather simplistic ideas that moral action and moral change are simply a matter of intention or will. We think, for instance, that after twenty years of using the practice of cursing that suddenly we are going to give it up on Ash Wednesday and we are stunned at our lack of moral purpose when suddenly, two days later, we find ourselves blurting out some profanity. For ten years we develop the habit of thinking poorly of one particular person. We relish these thoughts and on occasion we let slip to others these private estimations. Yet, with firm purpose we resolve never to think ill of this person again. But as soon as something goes wrong, we know whose fault it is.

Until we realize the importance of practices and how they affect us habitually we will continue the useless practice of making unattainable resolves. Those intentions will be nothing more than expressions of wishful thinking unless we begin to engage other practices that can correct not only our ways of thinking, but also our ways of perceiving and handling reality. Like the case of the cigarette smoker resolved to quit, we need to develop helpful practices to overcome the deeply rooted and long held nasty ones.

Four Insights for Moral Living

1. The decision to change a dimension of life always occurs in some context. While it is possible for a person to wake up and resolve without any previous reflection, "After twenty years of smoking, I'm giving up cigarettes" and to actually quit, most people do not and cannot change their habits so quickly. The actual decision to change is not usually a brand new notion. Anyone who has joined Alcoholics or Overeaters Anonymous, gone for help about spouse abuse or sexual compulsion, or sought therapy for low self-esteem or neurotic guilt knows how long the journey is – before taking the first step toward change. Like the seed thrown on shallow or rocky ground, decisions that are not deeply rooted inevitably have short lives.
2. Just as some persons can quit smoking with greater ease than others and just as no two people seem to quit the same way, we need to know that the path to change must be, effectively, custom made. If we really believe that God specifically willed each of us, then we must recognize our uniqueness as a condition for determining which practices are helpful and which are not. Appreciative self-knowledge has a lot to do with moral growth.
3. We must be ever vigilant against the belief that we have no need for improvement. We need to keep our

eyes and ears open to those near us who occasionally urge us on to greater growth. Appreciative self-knowledge without the willingness to listen to others leads to lives illustrated by those who believed that they had attained perfection. Too many of us are bullies, gossips, manipulators, or depressives to warrant such a belief.

4. We must know, as anyone in OA or AA knows, that each day we move from a nasty habit to a healthy one is due in large measure not only to our individual practices and the support of friends, but more importantly, to the grace of God, whose esteem for us is always beckoning us forward.

TWO

The Ordinary Moral Life

IF I ASKED YOU TO TAKE OUT A PIECE OF PAPER AND WRITE down three moral issues, basic issues in terms of importance, significance, and urgency, what would you write? Perhaps your list would include abortion, euthanasia, war, or divorce, since these are several of the issues we commonly think of as the moral issues of our day. Certainly they are important, significant, and urgent.

I would then ask you to turn over your piece of paper and this time to write down three things you thought of as you woke up this morning. List the kind of things about which you said to yourself "I really have to work on these." Consider how often during the past week you thought about these particular issues. Did you write about your personality? your work? your relationships? possibly one of each? After all, aren't these also important, significant, and urgent? Such issues comprise "the stuff" of our ordinary lives; the issues that most concerns us.

Now ask yourself: Which side of the paper is really about moral matter? My guess is that the very things you told yourself you "really have to do" are not what you count as the substance or central issues of morality.

Yet doesn't it seem appropriate that the specific issues of daily life that demand attention also constitute morality? Isn't it morally urgent to figure out how to keep from intimidating a spouse, to speak up to the boss, or to discuss a specific subject with one's daughter? Doesn't it seem that the sermon one is preparing, the basic needs of the parish staff, or one's inability to communicate with a particular young priest are also moral issues? Doesn't it seem that compulsive eating, angry outbursts, timidity, or self-doubts are moral material? Surely these are the kinds of issues we face day after day, and these constitute our moral tasks. After all, these are the matters you wrestle with when you ask yourself, "What ought I to do for Christ today?"

Morality Includes the Ordinary

Most likely the first slate of moral issues you drew up are grave concerns. Yet my purpose here is to affirm the need to think of morality in ordinary ways as well. We must think about the serious daily issues that grab our attention as well as our hearts and minds.

For the person who has a physical, learning, emotional, or psychological disability, the moral task is in trying to attend to the disability while becoming an integrated person in society. Similarly, there is moral material in the years many parents (mostly women) spend caring for children and in the years many adults (mostly women) spend caring for their parents.

We should reflect on two questions: (1) Why is it that we do not readily think of very ordinary, yet significant, urgent, and important issues as moral ones? (2) What ought we to do to engage better these ordinary issues?

In response to the first question, it seems that our readiness to associate the issues of abortion, euthanasia, war, or divorce with morality reflects a belief that morality is mostly about avoiding sin. Jesuit ethicist John Mahoney argues in *The Making of Moral Theology* (Oxford, 1987) that since the sixth century Christians have associated moral theology with sin. Then church leaders suggested that one way people could find out their moral status was through knowing what their sins were. For the next five centuries abbots formulated for confessors lists of sins with appropriate penances. Such lists became the way people judged themselves moral or not. The method in those centuries was not much different from the methods used in later centuries when other manuals, confessionals, and lists were developed.

Setting Positive Goals

Mahoney points out that, by contrast, Christians today need to develop a positive view of morality. We need not simply avoid sins; we need also to set goals and to ask ourselves what we ought to do for Christ, for our church, ourselves, and our neighbor. Mahoney is not the only one suggesting as much. The pope also is constantly exhorting Catholics to consider ourselves as acting persons called to greater freedom before Christ. To do this, we need to realize that morality is not simply about avoiding the wrong but is also about doing the right.

In fact, if you look at the two lists you made earlier, you would likely see that a major difference between them is that the first list is about sins to be avoided (euthanasia, abortion, divorce); the second list is about things which will *better* the situation you are in. The reason you have to talk to this person, work on that topic, or take care of some other task is not "to avoid sin" but actually to better your situation: you desire better relationships with your children, parents, spouse, staff members, pastor, or co-religious. The topics that were on your mind as you woke up this morning are part of your life's agenda by which you hope to make your own life and the lives of those around you richer.

Such positive goals broaden the subject of morality. Saint Thomas Aquinas attempted a similar task. In the thirteenth century most contemporary Dominicans studied a list of actions, mostly sins, (from the *Summa de casibus* of

Raymond of Penafort) as the text for preaching about the moral life. Thomas responded by writing the *Summa Theologiae*, where instead of writing about wrong actions he wrote mostly about who God is, who Christ is, and who we could become. About the latter issue, he developed the virtues, arguing that our major moral task was not simply to avoid sins or wrong acts, but rather to get into some healthy habits. (Ironically, however, a study of book sales in Thomas's day shows that the section of his work dealing with actions to be avoided sold more than any other part of the *Summa*!) It is possible to say, then, that Thomas had an agenda not unlike the one we woke up with: his involved the cultivation of habits and actions that would make life richer.

Human Acts Are Moral Acts

In response to the second question, Thomas offers three particularly helpful insights. In order to engage a positive and more inclusive way of doing morals, Thomas first wrote that all human acts were moral acts. No statement is more important for moral theology than that. It means that any act, behavior, or way of proceeding that we intend belongs to morality. The ways we teach, preach, talk, drive, meet, discuss, clean, etc., constitute moral conduct. We know, for instance, that the way we talk with our children, elders, employees, employers, neighbors, or spouse, is filled with moral opportunity to better (or worsen) life. We know that moral opportunities abound, which is why we wake up thinking about them.

Thomas' second insight was to focus attention on the fact that most of what we do primarily affects us. Although a sculptor or painter or carpenter or poet makes works of art, most of life's activities are things we do rather than things that we make. What we do affects us: if it is done well, it betters us; if done poorly, it worsens us. For example, a good run makes the runner run better. A poised dance makes the dancer dance better. And a parent's right decisions make the parent parent better. But strained running, sloppy recitals, and poor judgment worsen us. These activities (ordinary moral life activities) are what Thomas calls "immanent" ones. The effects of these activities redound to the agent. This is an important and wonderful insight, which says in effect, "we become what we do." It rings true.

If we drive to work like a maniac, chances are we will become more like one. If we treat patients with condescension, chances are we will treat our spouse, colleagues, and friends with condescension too. If we cannot keep confidences with some friends, we cannot keep them with others. In a word, we cannot think that the way we act now will not have any effect on us later on: we become what we do.

Finally, in order to become better and freer people we need to recognize and then take advantage of the many moral opportunities before us. Thomas suggested that we accomplish this through exercises; since every act is a moral one that affects us, then we should plan our actions so as to become the people we want to become before Christ. Exercising is what moral acts are all about. Thus, if we need to become more discreet, we should exercise discretion. If we need to become more courageous, then we need to exercise courage. If we need to grow in fidelity, then we must assume faithful exercises. These exercises help us to become the people we are called by God to become.

These insights from Thomas help us to understand just how inclusive the moral life is and what we can do to become more moral people. Above all they help us to realize that the moral life is more than important, urgent, life-and-death issues. Indeed much of the moral life is about the ordinary. Thomas tells us that, though we do not need his authority to convince us. (Even in our morning grogginess we were on to it.)

✵

THREE

Moral Advising in a Time of Uncertainty and Complexity

CONSIDER THIS SCENARIO. AN AUDIENCE OF PASTORAL LEADers is listening to a talk about moral advising in today's world. The presenter is a priest-theologian and the respondent is a doctoral candidate of theology and mother of three.

The presenter opens with a review of the upheavals, ambiguities, and dilemmas which the laity find in their lives today. He argues that it is important for pastoral leaders to have a firm and clear grasp of many issues so that they can advise with firm, clear principles and insights.

The student responds that better pastors are less worried about offering clear answers. They are concerned with understanding and appreciating the ambiguities associated with ordinary daily life. Quality advising, she notes, depends upon understanding complexities. Complex problems require attentive apprehension and response; grey problems necessitate grey answers. She suggests that discussing virtues rather than citing principles or offering solutions can be more helpful to those who seek assistance. Principles have precision and clarity, indeed, but for those reasons they lack the subtlety, malleability, and flexibility that problems of ordinary life demand.

Offering Virtues or Principles?

Her comments reflect well, I think, our own experience as pastoral people. The spouse who loses a job, for instance, hardly resolves resulting problems such as decreased self-esteem, marital tension, and economic hardship by hearing clear principles invoked. A conversation about the virtues of friendship, fidelity, or courage may be more helpful, providing a richer context for needed understanding and sharing. Likewise, the person who has been harassed by a colleague or abused by a spouse may find helpful a discussion on courage and justice, one that addresses the many conflicting feelings the victim is experiencing. The spouse whose loved one is on a life-support system with no real hope of recovery may look to the pastor for help, but the help sought is not specific advice about the decisions at hand. Rather, it is help that creates a context from within which the spouse can sift through the various options regarding continued treatment. Thus, the consideration of the virtues provides a context for dialogue between the one giving pastoral care and the one seeking it.

These and many, many other issues are often the "stuff" of moral advising in the rectory or pastoral center. This may come as a surprise, accustomed as we are to reading about the "big" journalistic issues such as abortion, divorce, homosexuality, or even birth control. Certainly these "big" issues affect many parishioners, but generally when someone asks to see a parish staff member, or when someone comes for spiritual direction, or when someone takes advantage of a Saturday confession, the advising they are looking for is a lot more complex than the question "to divorce or not to divorce," "to abort or not to abort." Parishioners' questions are seldom so singular, so focused. They tend to be as sloppy and as ordinary as human lives are.

Unlike the debates that occur across the front pages of newspapers, these conversations are face-to-face encounters between persons who are trying to find the right way of proceeding. In a nutshell, such encounters are, I think, prudential ones. There is a long history of such encounters.

A Brief History of Moral Advising

Over the centuries, church members have turned to pastoral leaders for practical guidance. In the fifth through tenth centuries, for example, Europeans seeking spiritual direction sought forgiveness for their sins. Desiring to understand the seriousness of their sins and the nature of the penances they ought to perform, they turned to the monks. Similarly, during the eleventh through fifteenth centuries, church members turned to the preacher of virtues and vices to understand better both themselves and the way of salvation. Later, the people turned to the casuists to learn what in their lives as workers, neighbors, and worshipers was permitted and prohibited. Finally, in the two hundred years preceding the Second Vatican Council, actual examples or cases were collected and codified into manuals, where under a variety of headings the moral seriousness of ordinary human activity was treated.

In each of these periods moral theologians provided guidance to local moral advisers. Moral theologians wrote the "Penitentials," handbooks that provided the monks with detailed categories of sins and corresponding penances. Thomas Aquinas and others wrote the *"Summas,"* which described the virtues necessary for the upright life. The casuists similarly engaged the cases presented to them by pastors who, in turn, had heard them from local workers or parishioners. Finally, the manuals, as legalistic as they were, still were more concerned with examining the material raised by the listening pastor than by the speculative academician. Moral theology was literally at the service of the church.

Advising in those days, however, was different from what is called for today. The penitentials, *summas,* and manuals were neat attempts to resolve the major questions a pastor would encounter. Each form tried to imagine the variety of activities a Christian might bring to a spiritual and moral advisor. Sometimes, pastors needed only consult the text to find the activity listed and its moral character evaluated. Of course, it was never that simple, but it tried to be.

Seeking Prudence Not Verdicts

These forms of assistance were as helpful as they were prudential. Prudential assistance to the pastor is precisely what they provided and to the extent they ably advised, they enjoyed circulation. They provided the pastor with answers, with lists of permitted and prohibited activities. But, given a series of developments over recent decades, such practices are no longer acceptable. Pastoral leaders are seldom sought to render a specific judgment or rubber stamp a decision already made. They are being asked to share their prudence. By prudence I do not mean the vice of exercising self-interest, as prudence has been considered (erroneously) in recent decades. Rather, prudence is the virtue of making responsible decisions. By considering and setting moderate and attainable goals for determining the lives we ought to live and by finding the particular ways of acting that will enable us to achieve those goals, prudence helps us take charge of our lives.

In seeking a moral advisor, the average parishioner looks for guidance in making personal, yet objective decisions. The parishioner seeks an enriching dialogue not in order to receive prudential directives but rather to grow in prudence. The parishioner wants to become a more responsible decision maker and believes that the acquisition of and growth in the virtue of prudence (responsible decision making) is facilitated by honest reflection on ordinary material with a prudential person.

There has been a major shift, then, in moral advising: before the Second Vatican Council pastors were called to provide prudential verdicts; today they are called to be mentors in moral prudence.

Why the Shift?

1. Living a morally upright life has become an incredibly complicated task. Consider, for example, how the family has been affected (and complicated) by shifting demographics; family enterprises have given way to the rapid rise of transnational corporations; family life is influenced by television and other media, as well as the accessibility of birth control, the women's rights movement, and so on. Questions of parenting, employment, education, and marital harmony demand an attentiveness to detail previously unparalleled.
2. Parishioners today receive much more formal education than in the past. Recently *The New York Times* reported that white Catholics and black Catholics are the people in the United States most likely to complete both high school and college. It would be unwise to assume these days that any parishioner's request for advice is a request to be commanded or prohibited. The education and experience of the parishioner stands against facile directives. The parishioner seeks the moral adviser to grow in prudence rather than in obedience. The parishioner seeks understanding in moral living.
3. Greater human rights and equalities, new democracies and the overthrow of oppressive structures have brought with them the self-understanding that adults are capable of guiding their own lives. Such insights,

however, are not original to the secular world. In the thirteenth century Aquinas wrote that to disobey one's conscience is always a sin, and that it is worse to disobey the conscience than to be excommunicated. In the twentieth century John Courtney Murray wrote in defense of the conscience, and Vatican II proclaimed religious liberty. Recently, the Catholic bishops have exhorted persons to follow their consciences. Civil and religious movements continue to develop in us the awareness that each individual has a conscience to form and to follow. That task is met through growth in the virtue of prudence.

If this book is to serve today's moral advisers, then it must deal with the moral issue facing the church today: how will we, the people of God, grow in prudence?

FOUR

The Christian's Call to Growth

HOW MANY TIMES HAS A SPOUSE FOUND THAT THE GREATEST trouble in a marriage is due to immaturity? How many pastors know that the most time consuming, enduring difficulties they have had is with a childish staff member? How many religious communities are held hostage by the puerile demands of one spoiled member? How many friendships are strained by the indulgent urges of someone who has remained the same since adolescence? How many of us know that our worst moments result from our own juvenile propensities that we have not yet faced?

The call to be a Christian is the call to grow. This seemingly obvious yet healthy maxim is not, however, readily found in the long history of moral theology. There we seldom find challenges such as, Are you maturing? or Are you becoming a better person before Christ for the church? Nor do we find questions asking, Are you doing enough? or Are you growing up?

On the contrary, the questions we are asked warn us against acting: Have you sinned by acting this way? Do you realize that in this way you may occasion sin? The theologian John Mahoney calls this "our preoccupation with sin" and remarks in his *The Making of Moral Theology*: "As a consequence of this commitment to spiritual pathology, the discipline of moral theology was to relinquish almost all consideration of the good in man to other branches of theology, notably to what became known as spiritual theology."

A primary concern with sin rather than with growth appears, for instance, when we define prudence as being cautious or being hesitant. Aristotle and Aquinas, by contrast, described it as being able to set long- and short-term goals. The classical virtue for growing, thus, has been redefined.

The Gospel Movement

Before looking further at the history of moral theology, let us look at the greater authorities on Christian life, namely, Scripture and the theological tradition. In the Scriptures, the call to follow the Lord has always been understood as a call to advance. Saint Paul writes, "forgetting what lies behind and straining forward to what lies ahead, I press on toward the goal for the prize of the upward call of God in Christ Jesus" (Phil 3:13-14). The ever moving Paul finds appropriate the imagery of straining forward on the way of the Lord. To the Galatians he laments their stumbling and comments "you were running well" (Gal 5:7).

Paul's reliance on journey imagery stems from his own experience of Christ, who literally breaks into Paul's life as Paul moves toward Damascus to persecute the Christians. Paul is a traveler, both before and after his conversion. After meeting the risen Lord, Paul is sent on the true way, but he still understands that all journeys require one to press on. Paul's actual journeys, narrated in Luke's *Acts of the Apostles,* mirror the Gospel journeys of Christ who heads for Jerusalem. Following in Jesus' footsteps becomes the disciple's call: the first traveler, the Lord himself, beckons each pilgrim to advance.

The Gospel story is replete with "moving" characters: the shepherds hurry to the stable as the Magi follow the star; Zacchaeus climbs a tree and Levi leaves his table; the woman with the hemorrhage pushes through the crowd and the paralytic finds the Lord by entering through a roof; the prodigal son and his father rush toward one another; Jairus and Nicodemus break ranks to see Jesus and Cornelius visits Peter. The Gospels are filled with stories of people literally striding in their passage to the Lord.

A Tradition of Advancement

The Scripture stories are not lost on the church's tradition. They become the source of a new moral imperative: to advance. Gregory the Great writes, "In this place one is never permitted to stand because unless one strives for the heights, one will slide into the depths." Saint Bernard, likewise, writes: "On the way of life, not to progress is to regress." Thomas Aquinas refers to them both and sums up their insights: "To stand on the way of the Lord is to move backwards."

Certainly this moral call to grow and to better ourselves is not a call to make ourselves into other gods. That was what those who ate from Eden's Tree wanted, what those who built the Tower of Babel wanted, or what those like the Bishop Pelagius advocated, thinking that by our own efforts we could become perfect.

Again Paul gives us clear insight: "Not that I have obtained this or am already perfect; but I press on to make it my own, because Christ Jesus has made me his own" (Phil 3:12). The call to strive, to grow, is not a matter of choice. Rather, Christ has called us and given us the grace that commands us to respond. On God's account, we must move forward.

Moral Theology: the Long View

The Vatican Council needed to admonish moral theology to be "more thoroughly nourished by scriptural teaching" (*Optatam Totius,* 16). During much of its history, moral theology evaluated sins instead of growth in discipleship. In the fifth through the tenth centuries, the famed penitentials gave confessors lists of sins, helping them to determine a sin's gravity and, hence, a fair penance. A person's moral worth was determined not by progress, but by sin. In the eleventh through the fifteenth centuries the scholastic theologians wrote their *Summas,* treating moral questions by comments on particular actions rather than persons. In the sixteenth to eighteenth centuries we find Casuists, so named because they examined "cases" of moral dilemmas. In the nineteenth and twentieth century moral theologians commented on their predecessors: writing in "manuals" they narrated whether casuists and scholastics achieved consensus about matters such as masturbation, birth control, stealing, lying, adultery, and divorce.

Even in the past twenty years the biggest debate concerns whether certain ways of acting are or are not in themselves always wrong, that is, intrinsically evil. If we read the penitentials, the scholastics, the casuists, and the manualists, we find millions of words about wrong acts and few words about good persons. We find thousands of questions about sins, but few about goals or striving or growing.

Early Preachers

There are exceptions. In the first five centuries of the early church, Christian leaders exhort us to follow the Lord by bettering the community and showing love to those in the here and now. They consider how we can walk on the way of the Lord while living in this world. These leaders – Ignatius of Antioch, John Chrysostom, Ambrose, Augustine, and Gregory the Great – give their moral instruction most often by preaching. Directly reflecting on the Gospels and the call of Christ they urge us onward. Centuries later, however, their successors caution us against tripping. The former want us to advance; the latter want us to stand still.

The preachers of the first five centuries are careful to urge us onto the *right* way. For this reason they appeal to the virtues. By concentrating on virtues or character building, they do not fasten attention primarily on pitfalls or obstacles. They attend, rather, to practices that can better the pilgrim. Though virtues assist the traveler to harness weaknesses and overcome liabilities, their overriding function is to develop strengths. The profoundly personal and positive emphasis of the virtues that we find in the early sermons on the Gospels stands in sharp contrast to the later obsession with sinful acts.

This connection between preaching the Gospel and invoking the virtues appears again in the great and challenging summons of Saints Dominic, Francis, and Clare to walk on the way of the Lord. Unlike the monastic lives of their predecessors, these thirteenth-century charismatic leaders enter the emerging cities and universities and preach the Gospel, forming religious communities precisely for that task. Telling the story of God's movement to us, they call us to move to God.

Thomas' Three Movements

Fifty years later Thomas Aquinas makes their preaching the structure for his monumental *Summa Theologiae,* dividing it into three parts: the movement of God to us; our responsive movement to God; and the meeting of the two movements in the divinity and humanity in Christ. Not surprisingly, then, concerned for the Gospel and for pilgrims' progress, Aquinas begins that second part with the powerful insight: "we may reduce the whole of moral matters to the consideration of the virtues." Aquinas like

Augustine finds in the virtues the proper mode of instructing those who read the Gospel.

At various points during the last hundred years, several moral theologians urged their colleagues to turn to the Gospels. Their prodding eventually evolved into the Vatican Council's mandate and more recently into a renewed appreciation of the virtues. As a result, moral theologians today are, I believe, more able to assist those who preach. By preaching and teaching the virtues, pastoral leaders and moral theologians can allow the boldness of the Gospel's summons to be heard again.

That summons is heard only by those, like the Good Samaritan, willing to travel the gospel road. Unlike the priest and morality teacher in the story, who crossed to the other side of the road, thinking it safer to avoid the beaten man, the Samaritan advanced and took the wounded man along with him. Jesus taught us the answer to the question, How do I inherit eternal life? It is by advancing on that same road Jesus took.

FIVE

A Dozen Questions about Conscience

1. What is conscience?

Conscience is the voice of God living in us which urges us to love God, ourselves and our neighbor. Through conscience we are called to judge our past behavior as right or wrong and to determine future courses of action.

2. Is conscience the same as the superego?

Not at all. John Glaser distinguished the two concepts twenty years ago ("Conscience and Superego," *Theological Studies* 32; 1971: 30-47). The superego is the term which psychologists give to that voice living in us which is a leftover from our infancy and early childhood years.

3. Well, what is the superego?

During our early years those who cared for us instructed us on matters of safety and hygiene. Our parents through persistent guidance kept us from running in front of cars, putting our fingers into electrical outlets, playing with knives or turning on the ovens. Similarly, they taught us to keep clean, wash our hands, eat with utensils and use the toilet. These instructions were given through voices of authorities much greater than we, spoken with great concern and often, understandably, with tones of stress and frustration.

When we were wrong, we were punished, most often by being sent to our room (shades of *Home Alone*). As the minutes passed we would sense a great deal of isolation and would want permission to return to wherever the family was gathered. We would negotiate with our parents, promising never to be bad again, and claiming to be contrite all along the way. Of course, we were not that upset about the wrong we had done; it was the isolation we wanted to overcome.

Through the superego, these experiences live in us adults. At times our consciences prompt us to develop ourselves more. For some this could mean a call to greater assertiveness, to others a call to vulnerability. Given that call to grow, we may hear another voice in us saying "You better not do it, or else you will feel guilty." That voice is usually the superego. Often the conscience's calls to growth are met with threats of the superego. When we do decide to develop in new areas, the superego still manages to make us feel guilty, and we feel terribly isolated. Some of us even go to our rooms, punishing ourselves exactly as our parents punished us years ago.

4. So are you saying that a "guilty" conscience belongs more to the superego than to the conscience?

That depends. When we say things like "I feel so guilty," we should ask ourselves, "Did I do anything wrong?" If the answer is yes, then the conscience is probably judging us, but when the answer is no the superego is probably intimidating us. For instance, someone has repeatedly treated us poorly. Our friends suggest, "You should speak up and tell that person to stop taking advantage of you." We believe our friends and acknowledge the situation, but the superego keeps saying, "You should be a nice person." Eventually we decide to speak up. Afterward, we may "feel guilty." This feeling is probably rooted in the superego: we went against its command to be nice and so it punished us.

Just as we can recognize the superego, so we should recognize the conscience. Our judgments that our friends were right, that we had to grow up, and that we had to confront the annoying person came from the conscience. As we grow up the voice of the superego and the voice of conscience often meet one another, sometimes in agreement and sometimes not.

5. Is the superego bad?

Not at all. After all, because of it we do not run in front of cars or play with the outlets and we do use the toilet and wash our hands. It is just that during our adult lives we have to live by a higher voice (the conscience) that discerns the standards of what is right and wrong.

6. But why is the conscience so important?

The conscience is important because through it we respond to God's call to be a person. We are obliged to become the person God made us to be, and the only way we can understand who we are called to become is through the conscience where experiences, standards, and reflections shape our understanding. Thus at the end of our lives we will be judged by whether we formed and followed our consciences or not.

7. So are you saying that we have the freedom to believe anything we want?

No. Conscience demands that we love God, ourselves, and our neighbors. Conscience is not a term by which we allow ourselves to do whatever we want. Sometimes it seems people use conscience incorrectly as a license to do whatever they want. But we have the right to follow our conscience only because we have the duty to form our consciences.

8. How do we form our consciences?

The most important thing about forming our consciences is that it is a lifetime process. We form it based on the morals we were taught by parents, elders, and teachers. Then we also listen to the teachings and stories from the church and sacred Scriptures. We learn too from insights provided by our culture. Our own experience teaches us a great deal as well. Finally, we learn from wise friends and mentors.

9. What happens if my conscience tells me one thing and my church tells me something else?

Disagreeing with the opinion of the famous Peter Lombard, Thomas Aquinas said that it was worse to go against one's conscience than to go against a church teaching. In fact, he held that we should even accept excommunication if that is what following our conscience entailed. Of course, few moral teachings of the church must be followed under pain of excommunication. Nonetheless, we are obliged to obey the church's teachings. If the church teaches one thing and we believe something else, we are obliged to know what exactly the church teaches and whether we still have grounds for disagreement. Then we ought to know exactly what the disagreement is and how serious it is, and to articulate to ourselves precisely why we are convinced that our way of acting is the more obliging way of loving God and neighbor than what the church teaches. In all of this, we must maintain a profound respect for the church's teaching and we must avoid scandalizing others.

10. Am I free to go against my conscience?

Never. Again Thomas Aquinas taught that if we go against the conscience we automatically sin because we are going against the voice of God. We have to ask ourselves, "If we go against our conscience what could we possibly be doing except going against what our conscience specifically commands us to do or not to do?"

11. But just because I follow my conscience, it doesn't mean that I am right, does it?

Not necessarily. As a matter of fact, when we think about it, it is pretty easy to get things wrong. To get something right we have to understand the circumstances and conditions, find the right means, and anticipate the consequences. If we miss just one circumstance or condition, guess wrong about only one of the consequences, or choose the wrong means, we are wrong. Parents, for instance, know well how often in directing their children their decisions miss the mark. But conscience is all we have and so we have to learn constantly through experience from our mistakes (and from our successes). Forming the conscience is a lifelong experience.

12. If you follow your conscience, but you are wrong, do you sin?

No. We sin whenever we do not strive to act rightly. Whenever we strive out of love to act rightly, we are acting out of conscience. Whenever we fail to strive, we (like the priest and the Levite in the Good Samaritan parable) sin. Sin is, as Jesus Christ taught us, a failure to love. And love is striving to find the right. Striving for the right, however, doesn't guarantee that we will be right.

If sinning is a failure to strive to respond to God's call or grace in the concrete, then we should distinguish between sinning and doing something wrong. On the one hand, we sin when we do not strive to respond to others or when we do not extend ourselves or when we do not try to overcome a vice of ours. On the other hand, there are plenty of times when we try to get things right and do not or when we try to avoid a wrong, but fail. We regret these wrong actions or errors, but they are not sins; they are mistakes.

13. (A Baker's Dozen) If that's your position then can't you say that Adolph Hitler followed his conscience and so he didn't sin?

That's preposterous. The conscience is the voice of God. As such it is the voice in us that asks us to learn more, to understand the needs of ourselves and our neighbor better, and to search for ways to make the lives of all people including ourselves better. Can we honestly believe that Hitler strove or searched in these ways?

Conscience commands the willingness to be open to God and neighbor. When we are not open, it's a clear sign that we are neither heeding our consciences, nor striving to love.

Questions for Reflection

1. Name four practices that you think are key to your particular state of life.

____

____

____

____

2. Do others in your state of life think these are the key identifying practices? Explain.

____

____

____

____

3. Name four practices that you think are a part of your occupation.

____

____

____

____

4. Do others in your occupation think these are the key identifying practices? Explain.

____

____

____

____

5. Name ways of acting in your life that you are taking steps to change or improve.

____

____

____

____

6. Why are those areas so important?

____

____

____

____

7. What practices could you develop for these areas of your life that you want to improve?

____

____

____

____

8. Name four qualities that you find in a person from whom you are most likely to seek advice.

____

____

____

____

9. In what areas of your life does the superego exercise greater control?

____

____

____

____

10. In what areas of your life does your conscience exercise greater control?

____

____

____

____

Part II

The Theological Virtues

SIX

Faith

A Journey to Dachau

From 1982 to 1987 I studied at the Gregorian University in Rome. During the summer, I would travel to either Germany or Austria, for part-time study and part-time parish work. One summer, while living in Munich, I decided to go to Dachau. I wanted to go on one particular Monday, knowing that like most European museums, the one at the camp would be closed. I wanted to go to Dachau only to pray, and I had heard that I could pray at a convent chapel that a religious group of women maintained next to the camp. In my Jesuit community in Munich, one of the members was the sisters' chaplain and he informed me that I could pray there, even on Mondays, when the camp was closed. Thus, I set out one cloudy day on my journey to pray at Dachau.

Foregoing a bus that could have brought me directly there from the train station, I walked about three or four miles. As I walked, I became more and more angry. All I saw were nice, suburban houses with manicured lawns. I saw no trace of the tragedy of Dachau. I started asking myself, How could anyone after 1945 live in a city called Dachau? What type of people did not mind having a mailing address identical to the place of such persecution? I thought, if ghosts existed, they would surely haunt this town. As I walked and could see the cinder-blocked camp ahead of me, I wondered how anyone could claim seriously not to have known about the killings. I got closer, the skies were dark and off to the side of the main street that led to the camp, I saw a new white, Alpine-looking church. I thought, who were these people who could claim that God was here in this place where they conspired to kill so many Jews, gypsies, homosexuals and others?

I got to the camp and was surprised by its length. I walked along its long cinder-block length to get to the rear of it, and rang the bell of the convent. I soon heard a voice telling me in German that the convent was closed. I responded that I was not a tourist; that I came only to pray. "We're closed," the German sister repeated. "I'm a Jesuit and your chaplain told me that I could pray here." "We're closed." "Can't I pray?" "We're closed; it's Monday."

I had come to Dachau to pray and was not allowed to. I began my trek back, even angrier than before. The skies were darker and my spirits were enraged. As I walked back I saw the white church again. I thought, I did not come to pray in the church where conspirers pray; I came to pray were the persecuted died. I will not pray there in that white church.

I thought, nonetheless, that I had come to Dachau to pray. Here I had an opportunity to pray. Should I avoid the very point of my journey? I crossed the road and entered the white church. I looked up at the altar and there I saw it. Suspended over the altar was an enormous corpus of the suffering Christ, crucified not to wood, but to the very barbed wire that the people of this town had once made. There was the suffering Christ, the Jew, and His cross had been fashioned by the Catholics of this town. They knew their guilt. And with as much speed as it took for me to see the barbed wire, I knew my guilt as well.

I had come as an innocent to pray for the dead; there in the church I saw that I was guilty.

I sat down stunned. For one hour I sat overthrown by my own guilt, wickedness, and sinfulness. I was awash in it. And yet, I did not feel any depression. I felt, instead, light. I felt that somehow Christ wanted me to know myself, my pettiness, my selfishness, my seething judgment and would not let me be shattered by the knowledge. I was overcome by my badness and yet Christ's strength, light and love would not let me be lost. I felt oddly confident, extraordinarily vulnerable, yet confident, not in me, but in Christ.

After an hour or so, I prayed for all the people that my selfishness had harmed. I begged their forgiveness and I thanked God for this revelation of myself and of God's tenderness. I left the church. Outside, I looked up, the skies were beautifully blue, with wisps of clouds across the horizon. Then a little boy passed by on his tricycle, saw me, and uttered the wonderful Bavarian greeting, *"Grüss Gott!"* He had just said to me, "God's greetings!" I sat down on the curb and cried. My prayer that day was truly blessed.

Meeting God

My prayer was blessed, in part, because I went to prayer as I really am. I did not go to prayer with nice words, thoughtful deeds, wishful promises. I went to prayer in anger, in self-righteousness, in invincible (I thought) innocence. I went to prayer, not as I so often do, that is, as I wish I was or as I believe myself to be. Indeed, I usually go as I think God wants me. I go to God with a made-up face, with a cover-up, with a mask. But God respects my freedom and does not yank off my mask. God meets me as I present myself. But if I am not true to myself how can I really understand whatever God offers me as I go to meet God.

Only by being ourselves does God truly touch us. Sure God can break through our obstinacy and artificiality, but God has always respected human freedom as is evident at the crucifixion, where God does not intervene to save

Christ or to stop us. It is thus in our freedom and in our vulnerability, that God touches us.

Generally speaking we think of faith as belief in God and, of course, it is. But Christian faith has a strong personal element to it, requiring that we affirm it. Faith isn't simply an utterance, but rather a deep down belief. Christian faith requires us to believe in God as we really are, with our whole being. Thus, the act of faith is the act of seeking to meet God face to face. I can only move toward that meeting if there is no obstacle on my part. Real faith requires, then, seeking the living God free of all artificiality.

In a brilliant work called *Till We Have Faces,* C. S. Lewis tells the story of an ugly princess whose father dies and leaves her to rule the kingdom. Her sister Psyche literally disappears with a fellow named Cupid. The ugly princess, in order to command the nobles' respect, becomes with great effort and discipline a powerful swordswoman. But so as to not distract her followers, she covers her hideous face with a mask.

After years of struggle and victory, the weary, anonymous and lonely princess learns that there is a temple of a god nearby, a temple that she never knew about. She enters it and soon discovers on the wall, drawings of the story of her sister's very happy life with Cupid. Angry that she has been alone with such a burdensome task, she shouts at the god: why did he allow this; why was she alone; why was she ugly; why did she have to be strong; why was her life so hard? She hears nothing in return and so in a fit of rage she cries out. She tears the mask from her face and again demands an answer. In removing the mask she realizes that for all the burdens she ever had, she never had the burden of wearing a mask before god. How could she meet god face to face, if she did not show god her own. *Till We Have Faces* leaves us realizing that the only one to whom the princess could have shown her face was indeed God. Faith should have let her do that.

We too often have to wear masks. For right reasons, we often suppress a part of ourselves, for the sake of our children, students, parishioners. For wrong ones, we compromise our own selves in order to win approval, friendship, respect, love. But with our creator, with the One who made us as we are, we believe that we can go as God has made us, and not as a fiction. If there is any place that there is not need for a mask, it is before God. There we live our faith as we stand just as God made us. Faith is authentic when we are.

Ironically, it is precisely when our faces are most in the need of make-up that we let our guard down and go to meet God face to face. As in my rage or in the princess' rage, we momentarily remove our masks precisely when we are not a pretty sight. When sadness, depression, grief, or loneliness hurts us, we turn to God, not victorious, but burdensome; not made up, but vulnerable.

Faith is that sanctuary that God has provided us where we can go as God made us and where we can desire to meet God as God is. For faith is that sanctuary where we can express our deep desire for intimacy with our Creator, Redeemer and Sanctifier. But that sanctuary, when we find it, is hardly a private chamber. Rather like the princess' visit to the temple or mine to the church, the sanctuary is filled with the narratives of others who have sought the same God with the same humbling truthfulness.

✵

SEVEN

Hope

IF YOU ASKED A YOUNG PRIEST AFTER TWO YEARS OF MINISTRY, whether he would prefer to preside at a baptism, wedding or funeral, I would aver that he'd answer, "Funeral." At weddings, the congregation's attention is all over the place: the bride, her gown, the groom, the parents, etc. At baptisms, there's the baby, the parents and godparents wondering what they are to do next, etc. In both the excitement is so high that there's difficulty with the focus.

Not so with the funeral. With funerals, the people's attention is caught up in grief. The funeral and burial are the final stage of a very long series of days through which the congregation has suffered. They are exhausted. In the middle of all this is the casket, a sure sign of sadness. The invitation to minister and to bring consolation is strong and evident. But to bring it in a way the mourners can receive it requires the priest to be attentive to the mourners' sense of loss. This is not easy: to be consoling in the face of loss.

As a high school student, I remember how a thirty-something neighbor of mine killed himself, how the widow and children came to our home that night, and how one of the priests of the parish came to comfort the family. Clearly, he wanted to console; he was there moments after the police called him. But, he was "upbeat." Too upbeat.

He smiled, laughed, and was very pleasant. He wanted to bring hope, but instead only brought denial.

Many liturgists acted with that same inattentiveness to mourners' needs when they reformed the funeral mass. In a phrase, they went from one extreme to the other. Before the Council, the praying church sat through the funeral mass for the dead. After the Council, we celebrated the mass of the resurrection. We went from grief to joy, from black to white, literally. The liturgists were right to want to introduce the mass of the resurrection, but they needed to introduce it into the context of the congregation's basic experience: a loved one's death. At a funeral the congregation is in profound sadness. To ask them to rejoice in the resurrection is not only unrealistic, it is inhuman.

The funeral liturgy is a liturgy of hope, not a celebration of joy. Joy is what Mary and the disciples had not at the death of Jesus but at his actual resurrection. Joy is what parents have finally at the birth of their child. Joy is what we have when we actually have something. Hope is what we have precisely when we do not have something. At a funeral liturgy we hope, at best.

At funerals many believers have a hard time of it. For both those who believe and those who do not, grief is present in abundance. But for believers there can be confusion. Believers want to know where is the comfort of faith. Believers want to know why they do not feel more the assurance of the resurrection. Believers wonder how weak is their faith that they feel as miserable as those who do not share the faith.

Many believers, distraught by the death of a loved one, are often not comforted but rather disheartened by their faith at a funeral liturgy. Here, in the wonder of the weakness of one's faith, is the meaning of hope. For hope is the willingness to not give up on one's faith, precisely when, in a manner of speaking, one draws no consolation from it.

Is the Death of a Loved One Easier for the Believer?

It is here that we ought to consider the rather odd claim that death is easier for believers than for atheists and agnostics. For all, death takes away as clearly, as physically, and as spiritually the life of a loved one. For atheists and agnostics death is the final closure; the door of one's life closes. There is no doubt about the meaning of death. Believers, too, sense the same finality of death; death is not experienced in any less dramatic way. Yet believers are not willing to accept the same certitude that non-believers have. In spite of the experience of loss and in spite of the weakness of faith, believers choose to leave the door of death open. Often, then, for mourners, faith does not comfort; it confounds. And that we stay with our faith is what real hope is all about. In the face of death, we believers choose to stand, albeit weak-kneed and shaky, before the promise of the resurrection.

If there is no doubt, no uncertainty, no disturbance, no wishing that we enjoyed more the gift of faith, then there is not much need for hope. But we stand in hope, hope for what we do not have: certain experience of the resurrection.

The icon of hope is an anchor. While tossed about, while adrift, while unsettled, we find in hope the anchor that allows us to stay where we are in our faith. Precisely when we are buffeted, hope helps us. Like courage, hope is a virtue of holding on, of tenacity.

Years ago this insight into hope was captured in a brave story by Brian More called *Catholics.* Set in a future time after Vatican III, there seems to be some discontent in a monastic community. A Vatican visitor conducts an investigation. Along the way we learn that the abbot, a good and honest man, has not been able to pray for years. Nothing comes whenever he tries. The depth of his struggles are made evident throughout the tale as he explains them to the visitor. Finally, in the film version, we see the abbot at night, terrified, alone, on his knees trying to utter the words of the Our Father.

The story captures the words of Saint Paul in his *Letter to the Romans.* There in Chapter 8 (one of his chapters on hope) he remarks that we hope for things not yet seen. (If we see these things, then this is not hope, he adds.) He writes that hope helps us precisely when we are weak. He comments that our weakness may be so great that we may not even know how we ought to pray, but, he says, it is at that moment when we hope to be able to pray (note: not when we do pray, but when we hope to be able to pray) that the Spirit speaks to the Father through our groans. Then, in our inability to pray, the Spirit prays for us, but through us.

In our groans, we hope. For our groaning is itself a desire (a hope!). To continue a dialogue even in the face of our greatest fears is itself an act of hope. Hope then is staying in the dialogue even when words escape us and yet the desire to articulate continues. Like the abbot, terrified on his knees, we too hope when we can do nothing more than express the wish to believe. This wish to believe is found in the hearts of many mourners.

Hope as Gift

And it is here at this moment that we must see hope as a gift from God. For, if we think that the tenacity of the grievers at the funeral, or the abbot in *Catholics,* or the readers of *Romans* are only hoping on their own resources, then we do not understand what hope is. For like faith and charity, the other two theological virtues, hope is not something we can acquire or develop. Hope, like faith and charity are gifts, pure gifts, expressions of grace itself.

Hope then is the Spirit entering into our tired, exhausted, fearful selves, offering us a way to continue the dialogue, to continue standing face to face with the living

God. Whatever enables us to continue to believe in the face of death, doubt, uncertainty, or fear, is hope. The ability to hold on, the anchor that steadies us as we are buffeted, is the presence of God in us.

When we see hope as gift, we see hope as God's concrete interest in us. But that interest is expressed precisely when we are at our weakest. Then, at our most vulnerable state, God's gift of the Spirit in hope comes. Hope is indeed God's gift to the vulnerable. It is only when we are exhausted, speechless, impotent, that is, in our vulnerability, when life is darkest, that God enters us to sustain us.

But the presence of hope is not bombastic or crude or rattling. It does not suddenly change our darkness into light nor does it turn our silence into eloquence. Zephyr-like hope is subtle. It respects our freedom, our intelligence, our emotions. Hope does not drive out our critical thoughts, our desert-like experiences, our deep rooted fears. Rather hope enters us gently assuring us of the presence of the Spirit in the midst of the turmoil. That gentle presence is strong, then, not in volume but in depth. It is the breath of the Spirit that comes as we groan, assuring us that at our weakest moment, without any resources, God will never abandon us.

✵

EIGHT

Charity, the Mother of Virtues

LAST WEEKEND MY BEST FRIEND WAS ORDAINED, A JOYFUL event in general and with one particularly striking moment for me. As my friend lay prostrate in the sanctuary, I reflected on all the struggles he had overcome to get to this point. As he lay in that humbling position, I thought about how humbling life is and prayed that he would rise from the cold marble floor a new man consoled by God's grace and charity.

I was surprised at my reaction, until I remembered my own ordination twelve years before. Lying on that same floor listening to the wonderful voices singing the litany and praying for me, nevertheless, I felt profound tension; I was not at peace. While I longed for ordination, had always wanted it, parts of myself were, as Saint Paul writes, "at war within me." Parts did not believe that I should actually pursue what I most wanted; parts were angry with the Church; parts felt I had no right to be a priest; and parts still mourned my younger brother who had died two years earlier. Still, I knew what I wanted and believed it was what God wanted, and this overpowered all the other forces within me and summoned me to ordination. When the singing stopped, I happily, and with real relief, walked toward the bishop to realize my deepest desire. Twelve years later, praying for another at his ordination, I thought, "God, this isn't easy."

To understand what transpires in the making of such complex decisions, we need to examine (1) how mixed our motivations regularly are and (2) how the virtue of charity enables us to follow the highest motivations among them.

Mixed Motivations

Many of us have moments or periods in life when something happens that engages every facet of our being. It is not that life becomes completely integrated or certain but that everything important to us seems to be captured in a moment. Couples on their wedding day, for example, may find themselves caught in an instant when the decisiveness of their commitment comes to the fore and "the war within" makes new and powerful claims on them. They could walk away from the altar right then, but most do not. Religious, too, before or during their vow ceremony, may experience such a moment, seeing what they are about to undertake in all its centrality and conflict.

Such moments occur whenever we see ourselves moving definitively in one direction and realize that if we continue, we shall be forever changed. In the glaring clarity of such moments we discover the complexity of our own motivations. Motivations, like choices, tend to be complex. We rarely act with a single motivation whether it regards the momentous or the mundane.

Sometimes we hear how conflicted or complex a decision was when the decision to be vowed, ordained, or married is in the process of being reversed. Or we hear romanticized versions about vowed life – "the idyllic certainty" of married persons, religious, and priests. Seldom do we hear the inspiring stories of people who, despite doubt and conflict, resolve to live a certain way and actually live by their resolve. Although the task of choosing a way of life that defines the course of one's future is enormous, many people make such decisions every day and stick to them.

The Myth of Pure Motivation

One evening in a discussion with students from MIT (Massachusetts Institute of Technology), I mentioned that we humans don't have pure motivations but can deceive ourselves into thinking that we do. Some students objected. They thought that business people may have conflicting motivations, but good scientists are animated by "a pure desire to know." Their view of people in business was a bit jaded, their view of people in their own field was disturbingly naive. I suggested that they might read about Einstein and Fermi, great scientists who never claimed purity of motivation in their research. We ended with a truce.

Certainly we aim at purity, but because we lack integration in ourselves, we lack it in our motivations as well. In order to bring those motivations into harmony, we need charity working in the depths of our being.

Charity

This view of charity may sound strange, since we tend to think of charity as the act of donating to appeals or as the virtue that urges us to help the marginalized. But charity is actually the virtue that unites us to God. Charity is not "primarily for others"; charity affects our relationship with God at the core of our being.

Charity is the most basic of virtues. Aquinas called it the "mother" of all virtues because all the other virtues are conceived within it. As the fundamental virtue charity is concerned more with the interior life than with the external act, more concerned with the heart than with the deed. Charity works behind the scenes. Unlike the virtues acquired through exercise, charity is God's free gift, enabling us to discover what is most important to us. Charity helps us every day to integrate the many motivations we harbor, affecting us at the deepest levels of life.

Examining the full spectrum of my motivations on ordination day, for example, gave me a glimpse of the complex drives working inside me every day. Charity helped me to discern and then focus on the call to ordination. Charity did this repeatedly throughout the years leading up to it.

Charity as Love

Charity also helps us to become more singularly loving. Charity subdues strains of self-centeredness, talks self-pity out of taking control, urges us to follow our motivations for justice and fidelity and to be vigilant against intemperance and cowardice. Charity is like a mother, guiding us lovingly but firmly to pursue what we love.

Charity is love, the very presence of God in our lives. As such it constantly sifts through our motivations urging us to go beyond wherever we have settled. Like a mother's love, charity's entire focus is extroverted. Charity does not tell us what to do in the concrete: prudence does that. Rather, charity moves us toward being more faithful and just, more self-respecting, temperate, and brave. Charity keeps working in the background.

Aquinas wrote that charity grows through intensity. He tried to explain that charity is deep within, moving us to see the one whom we love. Charity is about loving, about feeling intensely our love for God, neighbor, and self.

We grow in charity as we respond to it. Charity's daily urgings move us to be more considerate of an employee, to express more care for our family, and to face squarely our responsibilities. Charity is always moving us to become better people by growing in the virtues. Charity then is about pursuing what is central. Charity knows our many motivations and sorts through the strands, weaving together a variety of them. Ultimately, charity enables us to attain what we aim for. Thanks to charity, we can – with tension and conflict, yet, but above all with conviction – utter the words, "I do" or "I am ready and willing" on life's momentous occasions.

Questions for Reflection

1. Describe a moment in your life in which you felt and understood the presence of God.

____

____

____

____

2. Name four ways that you experience God as sustaining your faith.

____

____

____

____

3. What concretely do you hope for from God?

____

____

____

____

4. How do you know that Christ wants you?

____

____

____

____

5. What practices does God perform in you to strengthen your faith, hope and charity?

____

____

____

____

Part III

The Cardinal Virtues

✵

Introduction

FOR CENTURIES WE HAVE HELD THAT THERE ARE FOUR cardinal virtues: Prudence, Justice, Temperance and Courage. In a certain way of speaking there were really only two virtues, because temperance and courage existed to support justice. We were to be temperate and courageous precisely in order to be just. Prudence simply set the standard for what in the here and now was the just way of living, the temperate decision, or the brave act.

Here I want to suggest that justice does not stand alone. Basically I argue as I have elsewhere ("Proposing Cardinal Virtues," *Theological Studies* 56.4 [1995] 709-729) that prudence needs to guide us about justice, fidelity and self-care. Justice is about treating everyone equally. This is the virtue of fairness where there is no special treatment or preference. Fidelity is just the opposite. That virtue teaches me to treat specially those to whom I am more closely related: spouse, children, parents, friends, relatives, neighbors, community members, etc. Thus, while justice is about treating people generally equally; fidelity is about treating particular relations preferentially. The tension of the moral life is to figure out (through prudence) when fidelity is greater than justice or when justice is greater than fidelity. Good (and not so good) stories treat this all the time, for suspense is created when a hero or heroine must decide between justice and fidelity and therein is great tension. Consider, for instance, the movie, *Terminator II.* There Arnold Schwarzenegger is to find a young boy who is to save the entire world. But rather than go with Arnold, the boy decides to search for and save his mother, played by Linda Hamilton. The boy suspends the fate of all of humanity (the issue of justice) to save his mother (the issue of fidelity).

But just as we have general responsibilities to every one (justice), and special ones to particular people (fidelity), so too we have a unique responsibility for ourselves. Earlier, when I began writing these essays, I called that virtue self-esteem. Now I call it self-care. Self-care is broader in scope than self-esteem.

Sometimes we must decide among the three. That need to decide is what makes for even better stories. For instance, as the early Greek drama, *Antigone,* begins the city of Thebes has been nearly destroyed by a civil war caused by the enmity between two brothers. Both now are dead and one of them lies unburied outside the city walls. The new leader has the opportunity to unify the city and authorizes that no one shall take further part in the war, including even burying the dead rebel leaders. Should anyone attempt a burial, the new leader will put that person to death. The question for Antigone is whether to obey the law of justice for all or bury her brother and lose her life. All three claims come together.

The same triangular tension appeared recently in a movie, *The Scent of a Woman.* In a sub-plot, the principal of a prep school has been the victim of a terrible prank. Several students have destroyed the principal's car. A young man saw his classmates do it. The young man is an honor student for whom the principal had previously offered to write an influential letter of recommendation to Harvard. The principal learns that the young man knows the perpetrators and demands that the young man inform the school. While he realizes that the principal has a just claim, he also considers his need to be faithful to his (unjust) friends. As the dilemma develops the principal informs him that if he does not act justly, the principal will send a negative letter to Harvard, thus crushing the young man's future. Thus he must choose: justice, fidelity, or self-care. The lesson of prudence will be deciding the right answer.

In my schema, then, temperance and courage remain as they were, auxiliary virtues. However, they do not exist in order that we be only prudent and just, but so as to be faithful and self-caring, as well.

✵

NINE

The Virtue of Fidelity

IN ANY HOUSEHOLD WITH MORE THAN ONE CHILD A RATHER common dialogue occurs. First, after much yelling, shouting, crying, and complaining, the voice of a frustrated parent is heard, "Why can't you get along better with your sister?" Above the din, the tired and disappointed wish is expressed that one's children enjoy each other better. But the ever-resilient and resistant youngster, pleading innocence and arguing that the difficulty belongs squarely with the sibling, echoing the voice of Adam in the garden, responds, "It was her fault." Finally, the parent, with faultless logic, mutters the bottom line, "I don't care what she did; I just wish you wouldn't fight so much."

The genders may change, but the scenario doesn't. It conveys parents' fundamental wish that their children acquire an appreciation for one another. To that end, parents teach their children to enjoy each other's company through a myriad of activities. They play games with them, take them on family vacations and outings, help them to see the contributions each child makes to the family, engage them in family chores and responsibilities, help them to negotiate differences, train them to understand the importance of give and take. Through these exercises or practices, parents teach that the habit of being together is a happy one. In doing that, they work against the basic instinct of children to claim what they believe is their own; instead, parents try to get their children to see that life is better and richer where two or three are gathered. In light of these efforts, we understand better just how exasperated parents are when they cry out, "Why can't you get along better?"

Teaching Fidelity

Parents, the first moral teachers, instruct their children in the virtue of fidelity. That virtue is their "bottom line." By it a person develops and nurtures the affective bonds of any relationship – whether with spouse, friend, family or community member, colleague, or fellow citizen.

Until recently, however, despite parental efforts, the virtue of fidelity has received little notice from other moral teachers. Certainly we have been taught that "infidelities" are morally wrong; that is, we have been instructed not to engage in unfaithful activities. But when have we been taught to practice acts that strengthen fidelity? When have we been reminded to consider the moral activities of going to dinner with a friend, calling our lover, sharing a happy or sad moment with a friend, going for a walk with a colleague, lunching with an employee, or talking out problems with a relative? When have we thought that going to a birthday party, to the movies, to the park, or on a trip was part of moral living? Recognizing these activities as pleasant and social, we hardly consider them moral. For some reason, unless an activity deals with issues like fairness, justice, rights, or duties, it doesn't seem to concern morals. Yet to think as much is to lose (perhaps overlook) the force of the first moral exercises our parents taught us.

I propose fidelity as the first of the cardinal virtues that every Christian is called to develop. The others will be treated individually in subsequent essays. Now, after five essays explaining the virtues in general, it is time to begin examining them specifically.

Becoming Both Just and Faithful

Twenty years ago, the late Dr. Lawrence Kohlberg presented to educators a profile of six stages of development that could help chart a person's moral progress. The final stage belonged to the person who could recognize the claims of justice quite independently of the standards set by any society or individual. The goal for the moral life, Kohlberg effectively argued, is to become a person who can stand alone and recognize what ought to be. Certain figures whose moral authority is legendary: Jesus Christ, above all, but also Socrates, More, Gandhi, and King among others, appear to have achieved that goal.

Women scholars resisted Kohlberg's model. One of his colleagues, in fact, issued the most substantive challenge. In her famous book, *In a Different Voice,* Carol Gilligan noted ten years ago that when men and women are interviewed about who they are, a general tendency emerges: men tend to note what they do and accomplish; women generally describe themselves according to their relationships; both seem to be reluctant to act otherwise. Despite the obvious problems with trying to distinguish men and women by such broad categories, still, Gilligan raised an important concern. Implicitly she suggested that each person ought to have two concerns in life: one is to be just and to be able to stand alone to see the moral terrain for what it is; the other is to be faithful through relationships so as not to become isolated and unable to meet the other as friend instead of task. Each person then has two major moral goals: to be just and to be faithful.

Friendship: Key to the Moral Life

In the recent writings of moral theologians on the virtue of fidelity, two contributions are particularly noteworthy. In *Friendship and the Moral Life,* Paul Waddell recovers the teachings of Aristotle, Augustine, and Aquinas on friendship and demonstrates convincingly that in earlier times moral instructors understood the significance of friendship. Perhaps because we too easily think that being moral is something difficult, we presume that friendship can hardly be a moral issue. Yet once we see that these great thinkers considered friendship as the key to the moral life, then we may think of morality as a lot more human, attractive, life-giving, and, in a word, ordinary.

Waddell's research highlights an often forgotten dimension of the life of Jesus. Not only did Jesus teach and heal those who followed him, he also befriended them, called them together, played, laughed, and ate with them. His gatherings with friends were so noteworthy that they scandalized the teachers of the law. Yet, these were moral activities. Just as Jesus' life sets the norm we follow – being just as he is just – so too are we called to follow him in friendship – being a friend as he is a friend.

Margaret Farley explores fidelity in her work, *Personal Commitments: Beginning, Keeping, Changing.* She presents the imaginary lives of ten different people and examines how the art of a relationship requires a great deal of work. Farley makes clear that fidelity requires concrete exercises in order to develop. Just as our parents taught us through a panoply of activities to appreciate one another, so we need to engage similar ones if we want to grow in relationships. In fact, even to keep a relationship we must practice ways of communicating, sharing, being with, giving and taking. And like a parent's experience with children, we realize that such activities do not come naturally or easily.

Exercising Fidelity

These insights are similar to the ordinary, but frustratingly frequent, discussions mentioned earlier between parent and child. The parent's challenge to children that they accommodate their siblings is met with one child's complaint that he isn't being treated fairly. In the case above, the parent wants the child to befriend his sister, but the child wants his rights protected. The child's attraction to justice ought not to be underestimated. One philosopher, John Rawls, noted what every parent has already discovered, that the first moral phrase a child says is, "That's not fair." Curiously, a child's first moral utterance is not a recognition of what is fair; a child cannot determine that. A child can perceive, however, inequalities or disparities and cries out, "How come he got more than me?" Regardless of any answer, the wail of "That's not fair" soon follows. Trying to teach fidelity in that context is no easy task.

Likewise, trying to learn fidelity is no easy task. We find commitments arduous. Like children, we resent inequalities; we are suspicious of give and take; we enjoy control; we like counting what we give to another so as to be sure that we receive *at least* what we gave; we like to do things together as long as it is what we like to do; often, we share our lives with our friends, in a word, grudgingly.

Placing fidelity, then, at the center of the moral life invites us to engage in some concrete exercises and practices that can enable us better to understand and live what Jesus and our parents taught us, that is, to grow with one another. To this end we may need to make more calls, write more letters, cook more dinners, take more strolls, linger a little longer with a friend. We may also need to disengage ourselves from the habit of counting or measuring what "the other" does or does not. We may need to hush the wailing inner cry of "she (or he) always gets more than I do." We may need, instead, to listen to that more mature voice asking us "to get along better."

Fidelity in the Parish

But that voice is already heeded in many areas of life. Think, for instance, of the parish. In ordinary ways, fidelity is practiced by the staff member who is always punctual, by the usher who reliably assumes his usual task, by the youngster who shows up to serve on a cold, lonely morning, by the eucharistic minister who brings Communion to one infirmed, by the hospice worker who sits with a dying person, by the parent who shows up for Little League, by the AA member who sets up for the meeting, by the family that brings food to the pantry, and by the religious educator who, without recompense, teaches the faith.

I am part of a parish where, every May, the pastor sets up a tent on the parish grounds and hosts three events. The first evening he thanks more than six hundred parish volunteers by serving them dinner. Next evening he invites all the priests of the diocese to a cookout. The last evening he hosts a picnic for the entire parish. The pastor knows through practice that the habit of being together is, indeed, a happy one.

✵

TEN

Justice

IMAGINE A WORLD WHERE EVERYTHING YOU DO IS MONItored. Wherever you try to go, someone is at hand ready to stop you. Whatever you try to do, someone is there to say, "No." And whatever your feelings may be, someone else commands you to smile, stop crying, go to sleep, or play nicely. None of us could live comfortably for long in such a world of rule-makers, and yet most of us did for the first five years of life.

In those years when everyone else made the rules, we were powerless. Eventually we began to learn the art of negotiating with the rule-makers. We began by learning to ask the question "why?" Not since "Dada" and "Mama" did one word contain such power. With the "why" word, we were no longer passive recipients of rules. Now we made explanations of the rules a condition for obedience. The power-brokering "why" word may be the word that overworked parents most want eliminated from their children's vocabulary. Yet the habit of using it taught us as children that poor explanations often meant poor rules. It helped us to see that not all rules are right.

As children we tried our hand at making rules with other children. Generally speaking these attempts at practicing the art of negotiation with siblings, cousins, and friends were short-lived. Unhappy with the attempts, someone in the group usually decided to call the entire affair off, but learned the power of reporting along the way. "I'll tell Mom" were threatening words, words spoken when we, left to ourselves, finally decided that we fared better with the rule-making adults than with our peers.

Persuading and Negotiating

Sometimes we learned to negotiate with adults, such as relatives who baby-sat. Take grandma, for instance. With grandma to ourselves as the baby-sitter, we smothered her with affection. At the same time, we persuaded her to rely on her own more flexible judgment. Though our parents left the proverbial "strict instructions," we knew that it was in everyone's interest that grandma's leniency should rule the night. In our first foray into the adult world of rule-makers, we learned the force of persuasion as it plays into the art of negotiation.

Soon thereafter, when we would want to stay up late but our parents would not relent, we would turn to them and use our newly acquired bargaining chip, "But grandma let us stay up to see this show last month." Telling our parents that one of their mothers was, in effect, sweeter than they, turned out to be mighty powerful. Of course, we knew (too) that our timing had to be right.

There were baby-sitters other than grandma. On occasions, especially when the sitter wasn't a relative and was a teenager, the training ground for persuasion and negotiation became wonderfully complex terrain. We knew that before coming through the door, the sitter had three liabilities. First, if we were unhappy with the teenager, this baby-sitter (unlike grandma) wouldn't be returning. Second, the teenager (again unlike grandma) was baby-sitting for the money, competing against others as it were for our customer satisfaction. Third, the teenager was not exactly an adult. Unlike older persons with their established routines, we knew that teenagers were less boring and had as many likes and dislikes as we did. In our minds, this made for very interesting possibilities.

The telephone, ice cream, the refrigerator, boyfriends or girlfriends, cable TV – access to any of these was open for discussion. In seeking the baby-sitter's interest, we did not only want to suspend the rules, we wanted the baby-sitter to become a rule-maker so that we could enter into the process as well, creating new rules, determining such things as who gets to choose the television program, who makes the rules for the game, who should go to bed first, and who gets declared the best. It was our first time making adult-like rules.

If the baby-sitter resisted and adhered to the strict instructions, we did not despair. We waited from our bedrooms and listened for attempts to use the phone, rifle the refrigerator, or make some other move. Then we descended to utter powerful words: "We won't tell our parents." After years of experience, we had enough confidence to realize that unlike before, negotiating was more profitable than reporting. We would report *only* if the baby-sitter proved unreasonable.

As the years passed we learned more about rule-making and negotiating. Male or female we grew in practice. If we didn't trade baseball cards, we swapped clothes. We told exclusive secrets, we decided who came to which party, and we chose sides. As we tried to negotiate friendships, we often made a mess of it. We became disappointed, got into arguments and, at times, decided just to give up. But we were resilient and returned for another day of negotiations, perhaps with a new partner.

Acquiring a Sense of Fairness

Through these exercises in negotiating and rule-making, we learned that getting along with someone required not only good timing, ingenuity, persuasion, and reasonableness but also a sense of fairness. In any context, fairness was an unspoken fundamental rule. In fact, it seemed to be something we knew instinctively. As we have seen, a child's first moral insight is reacting to a particular situation with the remark, "That's unfair." Recognizing unfairness provided us with boundaries for knowing what was unacceptable. It may not have been well-defined at the time, but if grandma let a favorite stay up later or if the teenager was inattentive to a crying sibling or if a friend repeated a secret, we recognized the unfairness.

In fact, most of the Ten Commandments are straight forward prohibitions of unfair or wrong activity. We shouldn't be idolatrous or disrespectful; we shouldn't kill, steal, lie about others, or try to usurp what belongs to others. These activities are unfair. If we look at some of the great moral leaders of the twentieth century, we see that they, too, first recognized unfairness and expressed it, before they articulated a vision of fairness. Martin Luther King, Jr., saw segregation as unfair before he uttered his dream. Mahatma Gandhi opposed racism in India before he fasted for unity. Dorothy Day railed against the threat of war before she offered her vision of peace. Most of us are much more adept at recognizing injustice than proposing justice.

So what constitutes fairness? Is fairness making sure that everyone has a job? or health-care? or an equal opportunity? Is fairness sharing national wealth beyond national boundaries? Is fairness protecting peoples engaged in civil war? A simple yes or no hardly answers such questions. Rather like the lessons we learned about negotiating and rule-making, good timing, ingenuity, persuasion, and reasonableness will be needed to address the full-blown questions of justice. Still, we can only give answers if we have a sense of justice in our own lives, which we acquire only by getting into the habit of acting justly.

Discerning the Common Good

There are particular lessons that we learned through growing up which are applicable to this discussion. First, we remember that when we wanted to form groups or clubs we formed rules for admissions and duties for members. On occasion we realized that we were leaving some people out of our club. As children, we discussed these matters. Someone (I hope) in the group mentioned that it wouldn't be right to leave an individual out. Or, when we had birthday and graduation parties and tried to figure out who we could invite and who we couldn't, sometimes we included the child who was rarely invited. As we grew up we learned a bit about the art of inclusion, that leaving people out was not a pleasant experience for us or them.

Second, though at times we believed (and still do today at certain moments) that we would fare better if we only thought of ourselves, at home we learned that that belief played against our interests. We learned that cooperation was better than isolation, that give-and-take was better than grab-what-you-can, and that interest in the entire family's welfare was better than self-interest. Those nights when we successfully negotiated with the baby-sitter resulted from our acting on the premise that our welfare was as important as our siblings' and the baby-sitter's. And the lesson that our parents taught us, again and again, at the dinner table, in the backyard, in the living room, or in the family car, concerned the common good. It is the lesson that John Donne alluded to when he wrote, "No man is an island entire of itself."

Becoming a Rule-Maker

These two lessons of inclusion and the common good lead to another. Our utterances developed from the tenderizing "Dada" to the inquisitorial "why?" and from the "I'll tell Mom" to "We won't tell our parents." Our phrases matured because we were struggling to have a voice. We wanted to become a part of the rule-making process. As we did, we actually helped our parents to make better rules. Our input mattered. At first our remarks may not have been particularly beneficial, but in time they were. Thus, as we seek to include and as we work for the common good, our world cannot become more just if left to the vision of a few. Inclusion without voice is a puppet's role; it leaves both the marginalized as powerless as children and those who think they speak for all as deaf as before.

Gradually, we learned that being unjust was not a matter of being caught. As children, we believed that if we were punished we had done something wrong; otherwise, we had not. But since the time we became rule-makers, that is, since the time we developed our consciences, we learned that justice or injustice is not dependent upon what our parents or anyone else declares. Rather we realized that we were unjust when without justifiable and urgent reasons, we excluded or silenced someone or detracted from the common good. When we did not do a full day's work or pay a fair wage, leave a just tip or pay due taxes, we were unjust whether we were caught or not.

Justice, then, is not dependent upon the law. That a society does not outlaw an activity does not mean that the activity is just. Racism, sexism, and other forms of exclusion have been and continue to be permitted in many societies by laws.

As injustice is not about being caught, neither is it about whatever is outlawed. We learn to determine justice and injustice by developing ourselves. The more we act for the common good, by being inclusive and letting others speak for themselves, the more we can learn about the people whom we ought to become. Adults learn, as do children, through practice. Thus, the real key to justice lies in this: that inasmuch as we still have years to live, we still have more to learn about the virtue of justice.

✵

ELEVEN

Self-Esteem

FIFTEEN YEARS AGO IN A FRESHMAN RELIGION CLASS AT Canisius High School in Buffalo, I asked my fourteen-year-old students what humility meant. After hearing a few awkward attempts to respond, I presented a simple case: "You've just pitched a great game. Your neighbor comes up to you and says, 'You pitched a great game.' What is the humble answer?" Hands went up. I called on one student who said, "Ah, I was just lucky today. I'm not that good." The hands went down. The students knew the right answer had been given. But I said, "That's a lie, that's not humility." Now, they were completely frustrated. Another student ventured, "I'd tell my neighbor that the whole team is good." "Why?" I asked, using the teacher's tone that indicates to all students that they might as well not even try to answer that question. He tried, "Because I wouldn't be humble taking the credit." I shrugged off his response. Several other attempts followed. Finally, I said, "The humble answer is to say, 'Thank you.'" With that answer, these fourteen year olds now knew why their parents occasionally joked about studying religion with a Jesuit.

Making Humility Possible

Humility acknowledges the truth about oneself; it is not about lying or denial, but rather about the ability to determine whether what others say about oneself is true or not. As a matter of virtue, humility is the mean between two vices. Humility is found between pride, where one thinks oneself greater than one really is, and self-pity, where one thinks oneself worse.

I used to think self-esteem was a contemporary description of humility, a word so ladened with negative connotations that it seemed irredeemable. An essay on humility will never be read, but an essay on self-esteem will get reprinted. I've given up that idea.

Self-esteem is not humility, but the virtue that makes humility possible. If humility concerns how we interact with others, self-esteem pertains to how we live with ourselves. If humility perfects the way we stand among others, self-esteem perfects the way we see ourselves. If humility is about public discourse, self-esteem is about interior dialogue.

In her article "On Self-Respect," Joan Didion described what such dialogues are like. Without self-respect, Didion wrote, one becomes "an unwilling audience of one to an interminable documentary that details one's failing, both real and imagined, with fresh footage spliced for every screening. *There's the glass you broke in anger, there's the hurt on X's face; watch now, this next scene, the night Y came back from Houston, see how you muff this one.*" Without self-esteem, we are at once attacker and victim. Without it, there can be no humility or pride. Without a sense of self-worth, there can never be self-knowledge.

Years ago I concluded that the contemporary cardinal virtues are three: justice, prudence, and fidelity. Last year I asked my theology class whether I should add a fourth cardinal virtue, self-esteem. The hands went up again. The students, men and women, religious and lay, from twenty-five to sixty-five years of age, nearly unanimously responded, "Yes." One student after another pointed out how crushing ethics has been when its point of reference is exclusively social, as justice and fidelity are. "How many people," they asked, "who work for justice and fidelity play the Joan Didion tapes at night?" I responded, "Many." They agreed.

Four Cardinal Virtues?

Why name self-esteem a cardinal virtue? To answer that question, we need to recall that a cardinal virtue has three functions. First, it describes our bottomline moral tasks. Naming these four virtues "cardinal" means that being moral requires being prudent, just, faithful, and self-respecting. It is not enough to have one, two, or three; to acquire all four virtues is the goal of anyone who loves. Second, these are enough. As the word *cardo* suggests, all other moral requirements "hinge" on these four. If anyone wants to know what it means to be a moral human being we can say, "One who loves, which is to say, one who seeks prudence, justice, fidelity, and self-esteem." Every other moral demand finds its source in one of these virtues. Third, each cardinal virtue is sought for its own reasons. This last point conveys the importance of naming self-esteem a cardinal virtue. While we pursue other virtues for many purposes, we pursue a cardinal virtue for its own reward. Lack of that insight is the most frequent reason why we fail to acquire self-esteem.

Consider: How many times do we try to stop beating ourselves up simply because we are afraid that our best friend or spouse will reject us if we don't? How many occasions prompt us, embarrassed by our poor self-image, to add to our repertoire the threat that if we don't act better we will have no friends at all? How often do we press ourselves into a practice of "caring for ourselves" only to demonstrate to others that we can? When we practice self-esteem to get another's respect we are actually bartering childishly, telling ourselves that our self-worth depends upon earning another's respect prior to our own. We cannot attain self-esteem if we look for esteem elsewhere.

Sometimes we put unnecessary, even harmful conditions on self-esteem: we think it is permissible as long as the community's welfare, the workplace's environment, or the family's happiness is not disturbed by it. Or that we can regard ourselves well only if we hold our community or family in higher regard. When the family's happiness or the community's welfare is disturbed in any way, we suspend our right to self-esteem. How many spouses have suffered humiliations or blows in an effort to be faithful to a browbeating or physically violent spouse? How many employees accept the temperamental outbursts of self-aggrandizing and/or immature bosses for the good of the firm? How many young people internalize for the sake of the family what they think is their parents' "right" to prefer one child to another? Unless self-esteem makes its own claims to happiness – not based on justice or on fidelity but, like those virtues, on its own reward – then self-esteem will simply be exercised "when time permits."

Justice calls us to regard everyone equally; fidelity calls us to regard our friends and family especially; self-esteem calls us to regard ourselves uniquely. These virtues' three claims can be made simultaneously, leading to the fourth: it is up to prudence, to mete out the regard appropriately.

Teaching Our Children

The virtues are all acquired through practices. Through the practice of parenting we teach our children to be fair, to treat others as they would want to be treated, to include rather than exclude, to take time out to foster friendships, and to stand by those they love. By exercising justice we teach them that every person has worth. By exercising fidelity, we teach them that every relationship has worth. By demonstrating self-esteem, we teach our children their own worth.

Through our own loving parenting, our children see themselves as filled with love, with opportunity, with possibility.

We help children understand that:

- any feeling they have originates with themselves and that their world of interiority is as spacious as Central Park or the Grand Canyon;
- they are rich with emotional devices that alert them to be hopeful, happy, and dreamy when invited or afraid, defensive, and protective when threatened;
- while there is a world within, there is a world outside, as well. They learn, we hope, that from within themselves they can find the opportunities to negotiate the larger world as new and unique members of it.
- just as it takes time to understand their brother or sister, their friend or classmate, it takes time to know themselves.

As they think on occasion about us, their friends, or siblings, we encourage them to get into the habit of thinking about themselves. As we invite them to sweet dreams about mommy or daddy we invite them to sweet dreams about themselves as well.

Such lessons are as important as the ones on justice and fidelity. Nonetheless, while parenting attends to all three, the Church's attention to self-esteem is considerably less than it is to justice and fidelity.

The Church and Self-Esteem

One could argue that eight of the ten most important letters written by Catholic church leaders in this century concern justice. Also, homilies on fidelity – particularly, on family, marriage, and divorce – are a commonplace. When we think of Christ's constancy, Yahweh's abiding presence, the covenant, the Church's pledge, we realize that the notion of fidelity may be the most frequently invoked virtue in the Sunday sermon. But which encyclical tells us to regard ourselves well, treasure ourselves, and remember the importance of self-worth? Which homily gives us guidelines to acquire or bolster our self-esteem? What attempts are made to find within the Gospels the words of comfort that Christ obviously brought to those who came to hear him preach? It seems, at times, that a twelve-step meeting is the only place where a Catholic can find the importance of self-esteem constantly upheld!

We need more reflection on self-esteem. We need to remind ourselves that self-esteem is a cardinal virtue, that the moral demand to stop self-hatred is the same as to stop injustice. And the moral invitation to develop self-esteem is as urgent as the call to be just and faithful.

✻

TWELVE

Parenting and the Virtue of Prudence

AS I WAS GROWING UP, MY MOM AND DAD THREW GREAT parties on Memorial Day, the Fourth of July, Labor Day, Thanksgiving, and Christmas. Besides those holidays, neighbors, family members, and friends often came to the house for a cookout, to play cards, or just to visit. As my brother Bob and I grew, our friends began to come over too. Later my sisters and my youngest brother began inviting their friends as well. At any time of day, the Keenan house had visitors. We were neither rich nor poor, but we certainly enjoyed a full house.

My warmest memories surround the birthday parties Mom and Dad threw for Bob and me. Bob was born three hundred and sixty days after I was and so, as "Irish twins," we celebrated our birthdays together. The parties were incredible. My parents chose different themes: circus, wild west, etc.; my favorite was the Treasure Island party. Mom made a treasure chest filled with chocolate gold coins. Neighbors, friends, and cousins came as pirates and my uncle dressed as Captain Hook. I can recall him as he was then – one eye patched, hopping around on one leg. It was a party worth remembering.

When I was younger I never considered how much imagination was involved in my parents's plans. I thought everyone had parties like we did, though I never attended one quite like ours. But my parents' planning – their imagination and attention to detail – besides being an obvious sign of love and a wonderful occasion for joy, was a great example of prudence.

Planning as Prudence

If planning a party seems an odd example of prudence, let me appeal to experience. Almost anyone reading this essay is planning something: a family party, an anniversary liturgy, a class reunion, a parish gathering. Perhaps you are planning a program and trying to forge consensus or planning to begin a team and trying to select the right people. Perhaps you are planning a move or planning a date.

In planning we cannot merely attend to details; we need to foresee and to imagine. To make what we plan happen, we need to look forward and consider a variety of possibilities. Though people costumed as pirates or tripping as Captain Hook may not be appropriate for the plans we are making, our imaginations must answer creatively the questions about who should be involved – where and when and why and how.

Real plans engage imaginary future alternatives that we entertain in order to create a design that best carries out the task before us. When our imaginations meet the concrete in planning for the future, we become prudential. No virtue is more future directed than prudence. This may seem strange, since caution often comes to mind when thinking of prudence. But caution is needed for prudence only insofar as, looking to the future, we still lack the experience that tomorrow will bring.

Theologians have long talked about the visionary quality attached to prudence. Thomas Aquinas, for instance, wrote that prudence always sets the means for attaining the end. Aquinas wanted us to know that prudence is always seeking to make future possibilities become concrete. It is the virtue that leads us forward.

The German moral theologian, Klaus Demmer, puts it even simpler, "The moral life is not about being reactive, but about being active. We should see the situation before us not as something imposed but rather as an opportunity to shape." Demmer wants us to understand that the moral life is not about responding to what tomorrow brings. Rather, the moral life brings about tomorrow. And prudence sets its agenda.

The Moral Agenda

What is the agenda for the moral life? I have suggested in my last three essays that the moral life concerns fidelity, justice, and self-esteem; prudence puts these three virtues onto the daily agenda. The moral life is constantly challenging us to grow in the three virtues. For instance, through justice we learn more and more our need to treat all persons as equals. We understand better how our attitudes, intentions, and actions must become more inclusive and fair. We know that in some areas of our lives we are biased toward persons for any number of unacceptable reasons.

We men, for instance, are constantly learning how deep and ordinary our sexism is, and how we constantly have to acquire habits of recognizing and treating women as equals. To change ourselves we need prudence, which helps us plan new ways of imaginatively anticipating situations. Instead of finding ourselves in situations where we utter standard sexist remarks, prudence helps us understand that we have this particular tendency and that we need to harness it. Prudence also alerts us to the fact that we say what we think, thus, we need to change not only our words, but, more importantly, our thoughts. Prudence teaches us to overcome habitually poor reactions. It helps us acquire helpful habits of regarding and treating our women colleagues as equals. It brings us to reflect on why we have had such an unjust perspective and asks us to develop, in thought and in word, a more inclusive one. Prudence as planning, then, works on interior self-transformation.

Prudence plans situations that can change us. In turning to the future in order to change the agent, prudence recognizes that the problems of life are not that the world is unjust and unfaithful, but rather that we are unjust and unfaithful. If I am prudent, I will try to create situations where I can begin to acquire habits of acting more justly and faithfully.

Prudence as Parenting

Because prudence imaginatively seeks to construct situations for abandoning vicious habits and acquiring virtuous ones, I think of parenting as the best model for the virtue. This may come as another surprise because normally we think of teachers, clergy, or counselors as prudential figures, as people with whom we speak about major decisions in life. Indeed, on some occasions we need conversations with such people. But prudence is not simply about making right decisions. Rather it concerns being vigilant in looking for and creating opportunities for full flowering. That's what parents do. They are always planning the next situation for little Mary or Johnny.

Parents look at the big questions, such as, In what neighborhood will their child best grow up? or What schools will help their child develop? But often they have daily questions, such as, How does the child feel about herself? How does she feel about others? How outgoing or reserved is she? How does she respond to challenge? How can she better avoid running into walls or tables? How can she learn to be less shy but not too trusting? In the process, parents discover the uniqueness of their child. They realize that the child will only grow in situations that speak to her as she really is. And even then, most of those situations will be, for better or worse, probably unplanned!

Parents also know that they can't force their child to learn. Therefore, they provide opportunities where she may become interested in learning at her own pace. Parents believe that their child has a willingness to grow, but they realize their role in enticing such willingness. To entice her they must make the situation neither too hard nor too easy; it has to be new, yet not completely unfamiliar. The child progresses one step at a time. Prudence, then, requires not only knowing the child and providing suitable new opportunities, it also demands finding "the mean between extremes." Parents learn this through experience.

A parent learns, for instance, that he must watch his child always, while not protecting her too much; he must show great love, but he can't show it all because he doesn't want her to become overly dependent on it. Still, he must be sure that his daughter is buoyed by his love. How much is the right amount of affection? That's what growing in prudence is about.

As she grows, the father learns that he must be firm in keeping her from playing with the door, the sockets, and with pens and pencils, but he musn't be too harsh or too lenient. He must attend to the matches, the detergent, the expensive glassware – anything that the child can get her hands on and shouldn't. But what is firmness, and how does he stay between harshness and leniency?

These questions are a few of the many over which parents agonize. Parents answer them rightly or prudently when they find the middle point or that "mean between extremes." There's no secret code for finding the mean between too much harshness and too much leniency, between too much love and too little. Through the hard school of experience and reflection, parents learn it.

Parenting Ourselves through Prudence

Parents come to know their child, learn to create situations for the child's growth, and try to find the mean between extremes so they can help the child develop fully. These three points are key for parents; they are also key for the moral life.

If we want to transform ourselves into people of justice, fidelity, and self-esteem, we need first to know who we are as individuals and where our limits and strengths lie. As the parent learns more about the child through love, so we learn to know ourselves through love. Love always wants more for the beloved, however, and so we must look to the virtues to see where we need to grow.

Using as much imagination as a parent enticing a child to try something new, we need to plan situations in which the daily possibility for growth becomes real. Becoming more just, faithful, and self-respecting is a lifelong task, thus, each of us needs to learn how to grow at a bearable pace. Some of us may have spent years developing an appreciation for the common good, but our experience with relationships has suffered. To learn later in life the virtue of fidelity will be an awkwardly slow task. Others may encounter the same awkward slowness as they discover how just and faithful they are, but how miserably low their self-esteem is.

To move forward, then, we can lead ourselves as a parent leads a child: appreciating our uniqueness, anticipating the next steps, and patiently but continuously guiding ourselves so that we do not tire of the nearly endless journey that lays before us in acquiring the virtues. Along the way, the imagination that helps us to plan and execute the journey will be our most prudential asset.

✵

THIRTEEN

Courage

TODAY'S CARDINAL VIRTUES ARE JUSTICE, FIDELITY, SELF-esteem, and prudence, each of which I have treated in earlier essays. The first three direct us to treat all persons equally, helping us sustain and develop relationships, and to regard ourselves with self-respect. Prudence tells us what justice, fidelity, and self-esteem mean in the concrete. But two other virtues, courage and temperance, are also needed if we want to act continuously with virtue. These are instrumental virtues, that is, they exist so that we can be just, faithful, self-respecting, and prudential.

Conviction Anchors Courage

One night when my Dad, a police officer, was working, my Mom woke me, saying she thought she had heard someone in the basement. She said it was probably just the house "settling," but to be certain, she asked if I would go down with her to see that the house was secure. "Sure," I said, but I was frightened. As we returned from the basement, she thanked me and told me that I was brave. It seemed an odd remark in light of my own fear: if I was so brave, why was I so afraid? When I told her my dilemma, she said that being brave doesn't mean "not being afraid"; it means still doing what one has to do, despite fear.

As a kid growing up in Brooklyn, I had thought being brave was like "being tough," and that being courageous meant showing no fear – to be courageous was the opposite of being a sissy. Many people, I think, mistake fearlessness for courage; they envision G. Gordon Liddy holding his hand over a flame. My mother's remark, however, pointed me toward something different.

Consequently, I began to notice persons who did what they had to do even when they were afraid. There were the nuns marching in Selma. While I didn't understand at the time why they weren't in the classroom teaching, I still thought they were brave. There they were being insulted and yelled at. In Brooklyn, I thought, no one would dare do that. The Sisters went to Selma, aware that they "were asking for trouble." I realized even then that they were doing what they had to do, because on their placards and in their faces was conviction.

When I saw the television footage, showing hoses and dogs being used against African Americans marching for civil rights, I realized how brave those people were. They *knew* they were going to be hurt, and they *still* went forward. These people began to convince me that such behavior was important.

Years later came a similar scene in the movie "Gandhi" – men walking up to the police knowing that their heads would be smashed; none were looking to fight, and all were, I'm sure, frightened; yet they stood firm against people stronger than they.

Conviction provides the anchor for understanding courage. The brave remain steadfast with their convictions, even in face of threat or loss. Conviction applies to more than the brave who champion justice. The brave mountaineer, explorer, or navigator is brave not because she wrestles and subdues her fear, but rather because in the face of adversity she maintains her course; she continues steadfast with the conviction that she must complete her journey. She stays resolved. Standing firm with one's convictions seems to underlie courage.

Standing firm is, of course, a metaphor for not capitulating. Rosa Parks stood firm when she took a seat in the front of a bus. Thomas More stood firm as he sat in prison refusing to sign the King's oath. Such persons were set with conviction and rather than capitulate to rational fear, they stood firm.

The Courageous Rush In and Reach Out

The metaphor can be overstretched, however, when we think of occasions when someone runs into a burning building to save another, or defends a person being attacked, or hurries to another's aid. Here the courageous one does not stand firm; quite the contrary, in a time of emergency, the courageous one is precisely the one who moves.

The significance of this movement cannot be underestimated. Aristotle reminds us that one's true moral character is revealed in spontaneous situations. In an emergency, the courageous and the coward are more visible: whenever we have to act, without time to deliberate, we generally reveal whether our instincts are baser or better than they normally appear. Admittedly the emergency is exceptional, but it still presents an arguably adequate context for understanding moral courage. In each instance, courage is seen when one person reaches out to another in need in the face of danger, the quintessential act of the brave rescuer.

On further reflection, we see similarities between those who stand firm and those who rush to the rescue:

- In both instances, adversity threatens – whether it is racial oppression, brute force, a storm, or a fire.

- Against difficulty the brave struggle to keep the situation from worsening, either by staying the course or by moving quickly.
- In both cases, the courageous one believes that he specifically is capable of keeping the situation from worsening; otherwise, he would be reckless. Thus, if strikers suffered head beatings or hosings without any measure of hope of drawing attention to their oppressors, then their acts would be irresponsible. Similarly, if there were probable certitude that the rescuer would become incapacitated in the attempt, then he would, in effect, worsen the situation.
- In all the cases of rescue (and many of standing firm), the courageous are in solidarity with the vulnerable – whether trapped in a building or in an oppressive regime. Both ultimately weigh personal danger against the cost of abandonment.

These two stances, standing firm and reaching out, seem to be complementary expressions of the same reality: the courageous person is unwilling to abandon the person or principle endangered. True courage is the virtue of one who refuses to abandon in the face of threat.

The Courage at Calvary

Defined in this way, much of the bravery of the Scriptures becomes apparent. The bravery of Christ in the Garden is found not only in his willingness to accept the cross, but that he accepts it precisely so as not to abandon the will of his Father, which is to save us. The Incarnation, Passion, and death of Jesus is, then, the ultimate act of rescue. His bravery is mirrored in the bravery of Mary his mother, John the disciple, Mary Magdalene. and the other women who stand firm at the cross and do not, like the other disciples, abandon him. The courage shown at Calvary is a definitive moment in human history.

Not surprisingly, soldiers have found the face of courage in the cross and in the Johannine phrase "No greater love than this. . . ." The face of courage is found not by overcoming one's fears but by confronting one's humanity as it is threatened. The soldier goes to war to defend; his courage lies in his refusal to abandon his country in need. But in the war, where he is called to stand firm and defend the homeland in the face of great adversity, there is also the call, on occasion, to rescue. The courageous soldier becomes a hero when he reaches out to a civilian or another soldier left behind. Wartime heroism is the story of brave defenders courageously engaged in rescue operations. Bravery in war is not wrestling with fear; it is saving life.

Developing Courage

But how do we develop courage? To answer, consider the exercises of soldiers, who like the police, require courage as an essential virtue for the vocation: to maintain the peace at home and elsewhere. This role incorporates both stances of courage, to stand firm and defend and to go into combat when necessary.

The willingness to be at the forefront of the nation's defense is a clear manifestation of a soldier's courage. But that courage does not move him to create risk, confrontation, or danger. The courageous soldier does not instigate conflict, but reacts to threat. Courage is always a responsive attitude; it does not look for trouble but helps defend, protect, or rescue when someone or something else threatens.

The disposition to protect becomes a virtue when perfected by prudence and solidarity. Brave soldiers are trained to be prudent – to be prepared and alert to the possibility of difficulty and threat. Taught to be smart practically, the soldier assesses dangers, outcomes, and risks.

The disposition toward courage must be coupled with an understanding of how to anticipate and subdue threat.

Throughout training the soldier is also instructed in solidarity. She learns to think of herself never as a lone agent but, like it or not, always as a member of a troop, a company, a battalion. The soldier alone does not subdue the threat; only the troops, as a single entity, do. Thus, the military fosters a strong sense of interdependence, while highlighting the viciousness of abandonment. The military instills in the soldier the recognition that one stands firm together.

The willingness to face threat is perfected into a virtue by prudence and solidarity. Thus, the soldier who seeks to prove his bravery is exactly what the military rejects, for vanity, like insecurity, is neither prudent nor dependable. In conflict, the soldier's bravery becomes heroism when the balance of solidarity over prudence tilts, and the soldier reaches out to a comrade or civilian dangerously left behind. Wartime heroism is when brave defenders rescue against the odds. That said, heroism and recklessness are precisely differentiated in that the hero is normally accustomed to prudence. In the brave soldier, prudence and solidarity are generally inseparable.

Preparedness

Short of war games, we cannot construct imaginary settings in which we can exercise courage. Courage does not develop by preplanned exercises; and, unlike virtues such as fidelity, justice, or temperance, it does not enjoy a repertory of programs that help us to grow. This is because courage is what Aquinas called the reactive virtue: it only acts in the face of threat.

What we can do is exercise preparedness. We can teach one another to stand firm. As in the military, such exercises are designed to build up our solidarity with one another. For this end, justice and fidelity are the virtues that help us to constitute that solidarity. They develop our appreciation of the equality of all, as well as deepen our relationships with family, friends, and neighbors. They give us a firmer hold on one another and help us in those moments when the temptation to abandon in the face of threat arises.

But sometimes we need to develop a sense of our own worth so that we may reasonably defend ourselves against threats. This willingness is rooted in self-esteem. The person who has been endangered, initimidated, and humiliated by bullies may claim her dignity by standing firm in solidarity with true friends, refusing to surrender to another round of abuse. The person fighting an addiction or a compulsion, who has repeatedly abandoned his own dignity and surrendered to threatening fears, must claim his self-possession, standing firm and refusing to give up.

Rooted in the Latin word for heart, *cor,* courage is deepened as our humanity is more profoundly rooted in justice, fidelity, and self-esteem. It is exercised whenever we stand firm, whenever we stretch forward, and whenever, concerned about the rest who are asleep, we respond to noises and pass quietly down those steps to make things secure. Whether practiced by a soldier defending his country, by a parent protecting her children, or by a nun standing firm against racism, it is always apparent when people love their humanity enough to defend it.

❋

FOURTEEN

Temperance

WHEN I TAUGHT MORAL THEOLOGY TO THE UNDERGRADUATES at Fordham University we discussed the virtues. In presenting the first virtue, temperance, I proposed the following case: "Suppose your roommate habitually parties a great deal with two friends. If you were to tell him that he was partying too much, what do you think he would do?" They all gave the same response: "He would probably ask the two friends whether he parties too much." That response was particularly insightful.

Often, when someone questions our behavior (about eating, drinking, or working too much or too little) we, too, tend to seek the opinion of the very people who share the same behavior. Our second opinion is usually a safe one.

Habits and Habitues

The Fordham students, however, were open to self-examination. In their early twenties, they were just learning the importance of temperance. Although they had better eating, drinking, working, and sleeping habits than I did when I was their age, still, they needed to improve. After all, some of them developed the oddest sleeping habits, some let their papers go to the last minute, others went on reckless diets, and a few drank too much. Most of them realized that they would have to give up wrong habits to acquire right ones.

They weren't only learning personal habits, however. They were also getting accustomed to the art of attending social gatherings – learning how to drink, develop relationships, and grow responsibly. As they did, they helped one another. Unfortunately, those who were not successful, like the student who partied too much, often fell out of a circle of friends who could have been helpful. While some were acquiring new and right habits, others were not. In time, the students had begun frequenting one of two different types of parties: those where few drank too much, and those where everyone did.

Most of us who suffer intemperance in some area of life find ourselves isolated from people who are temperate. If we have an eating disorder, we engage it when no one is around. If we drink too much, we do it either with those who are equally isolated or, worse, when no one knows. If we suffer some sexual compulsion, we act on it covertly. Because secrecy surrounds intemperance, intemperance and isolation are familiar bedfellows.

Step 1: Admitting the Problem

Like the student who parties too much, the intemperate adult is reluctant to leave the privacy of isolation to improve upon intemperate ways. For this reason, in the series of steps needed to acquire temperance the proverbial "first" is the simple admission that one has a problem. The truth is, by admitting the problem one overcomes the reluctance to face personal shortcomings. Moreover, any admission like this means that one is trying to reveal the secret, to come out of one's private world, to leave the isolation. When we admit to having a problem we are trying to break free of a world of darkness, of self-deception, and of terrible loneliness. When we admit our problem, we try to enter the real world.

Step 2: Finding the Right Person

Like someone who has been hidden away or abandoned we are usually quite vulnerable when we make the admission. For this reason the second step to acquiring virtue is equally important: finding the right person with whom to talk. Shedding the vice and acquiring the virtue requires talking with the right people. Yet, often we don't know the right people, people who are familiar with the difficulties we have and also capable of advising us.

Finding the right person (or people) to talk with can be daunting. My students, for instance, remarked that if the fellow who partied too much finally decided to talk with someone, there was a good probability that he would talk with someone at the other end of the spectrum, in his case, somebody who never goes to parties. When I asked "Why?" they answered, "because he is trying to find someone more reliable to talk with." "But why wouldn't he realize that this person would not be that helpful?" "Because while he has no friends who know how to enjoy a party, at least this person doesn't get drunk regularly."

Like the student, we may turn to someone who does not make the mistakes we do, but who doesn't have any experience either. It is important to realize that the right person is somewhere inbetween.

Certainly anyone familiar with twelve-step programs for drinking, eating, sexual, or work compulsions knows the importance of talking with the right person, as does anyone who has joined a support group. In fact, everyone needs to learn how to find prudential advisors because the virtue of temperance is difficult to acquire.

Step 3: Finding the Right Exercises

Unfortunately, when we think of temperance we tend to think singularly of abstinence. Certainly, temperance often requires us to be abstinent in one or two particular areas of life. For instance, we may have to abstain from drinking if drinking temperately means always "having to have" a drink. Nonetheless, temperance concerns many more activities than drinking. It usually requires us to achieve a balance between too little and too much of the activity, rather than abstaining from it completely.

Like any other virtue, temperance is about bettering ourselves. To do that we need to do a series of exercises. The word "exercise" is appropriate. The Arab philosopher Avicenna used it to talk about the virtues and Thomas Aquinas later adopted it as well. Like the students who need to learn right sleeping, eating, drinking, and working exercises to develop right habits, we, too, need the right exercises to develop temperance.

a. Seeking Tension. Consider the analogy of body building. We can only begin to advance if we know how much weight we can lift. Beginners often start by taking on too much weight, and end up pulling a muscle, unable to workout for a while. It is also possible to err by overdoing exercises in temperance. Body builders must know not only the weights that are too heavy, but those that are too light. Anyone who can lift a weight easily knows that there will be little benefit: muscles only grow when there is tension. Gauging the tension between "almost too much" and "almost too little" is the real key to body building.

b. Acquiring Balance. The tension pertains not only to the amount of weight we lift, but also to how we lift. Beginners usually favor one side, arm, or leg over another, lifting unevenly. The novices usually needs a year of lifting to attain the right balance.

A similar combination of tension and balance is needed to develop temperance. Without significant challenge, we stand little chance of growth. When we were younger, we thought it would be easier to stay or to become trim. Of course, we wished we could stay up as late as we wanted without disturbing our productivity, too! We thought our affections for others could be easily expressed.

We fervently believed we could overcome our internal insecurities simply by ignoring them. But our temperaments, like our bodies, tend to remain as they are unless we engage in demanding exercises. Unless we stretch ourselves, our temperaments will stay exactly as they are.

c. Achieving Integration. In acquiring the virtue of temperance, we may find that we have some strengths and some weaknesses. We may favor our strengths and ignore our weaknesses, but if we do we won't grow in temperance. Like body building, temperance concerns the whole person. In fact, temperance is really only a virtue when it achieves integration.

d. Maintaining Consistency and Endurance. The gains in body building depend not only on balance and tension, but on consistency and endurance. Just as it takes a year to be able to do regularly "balanced" lifts and presses, the gains in acquiring virtue are slow. Consistent commitment is a necessity. Moreover, unless we continue to exercise, our muscles lose their tone and strength and eventually atrophy. Because our temperaments are so set, momentary exercises, regardless of their intensity, leave only momentary effects. Consistent exercises of temperate behavior are a lifelong task.

Temperance, like body building, is not an end in itself but an aid toward other ends. Temperance gives us the strength we need to do a number of tasks. Temperance is a helping virtue that makes us capable of living out the four cardinal virtues – prudence, justice, fidelity, and self-esteem. Without temperance, the four virtues would be more like wishes than achievable goals.

Step 4: Enjoying the Exercises

As a virtue, temperance is, as Aristotle says, its own reward. Temperance is about enjoying life. It is about our being able to experience our temperaments as best we can.

Aristotle noted that temperance is about sensibility, finding a balance within ourselves so that all our sensibilities can flourish. He rightly believed that to be balanced is to be happy. His notion of balance was a creative one, not a controlled one.

We are temperate people when we hit our stride. Temperance is living the life of constant exercises that keep all our sensibilities, feelings, inclinations, hungers, and urges well toned and tuned.

The growth of the temperate person, like that of the body builder, has its sensual and visceral affects. Temperance is, after all, the development of ourselves as "sensible" people. And rather than shy away from it, Catholics have special reason to be attracted to it. Our faith is especially inclined to the physical. We believe, for instance, that the second person of the blessed Trinity became flesh, that we eat Christ's body and drink his blood, that eternal life is the resurrection of our bodies, and that our church is rightly called the body of Christ. Whether we talk about the Incarnation or the Eucharist, about resurrection or the church, the language of our faith is very physical. (Consider, for instance, that the most significant political act in our church life, the election of the pope, occurs in a room famous for its frescoes of nude bodies!)

Certainly, many people think that temperance is the virtue that keeps us from getting worse: it stops us from being drunk, obese, or sluggish. But the real meaning of temperance is not found in what it prevents, but in it what it provides. Temperance provides a foretaste of eternal life, with a sense of integration and well-being, where we find happiness by finding our stride.

Of course, that happiness is not our final end; Christ is our final end. But through temperance we learn to savor what it means to be human, what it means to be in God's image. When we allow our temperaments to be challenged, balanced, and stretched for the sake of the cardinal virtues, we discover from within an enjoyable hint of the promise in store for us. That promise is found in the sentiments of Saint Augustine, that the glory of God is the human "fully alive."

✵

FIFTEEN

The Virtues and the Imagination

TWELVE YEARS AGO, AS A STUDENT AT THE GREGORIAN University in Rome, I began looking for a new type of moral theology. I felt that moral theology was being rent in two by an argument over intrinsic evil, an argument, that struck me as more about whether artificial birth control was an intrinsic evil than *whether* there was any intrinsic evil. Moral theologians were caught in an intractable debate that would never allow them to achieve consensus. Rather than entering it, I began to imagine some type of moral theology that talked less about specific actions and more about persons. I sought an agenda that considered not only momentous activities like divorce, abortion, and murder but also daily concerns of lesser magnitude.

In particular, I dreamed of something positive, a moral theology that while preventing people from becoming worse, also helped them to become better. Where was the moral theology that could help ordinary people – secretaries, bankers, housewives, carpenters, investigators, and restaurant managers – set goals and guidelines for their lives? I mused about a moral theology that could breathe the breath of the Gospels, one that expressed the parables of the Good Samaritan and the Prodigal Son. I wanted a moral theology that depended on the stable, the mount, the hill, the tomb and the upper room. I searched for a method in moral theology that could help preachers preach and spiritual directors direct and a form of moral theology that was rooted in the tradition, while still being fresh for the end of the twentieth century.

I also hoped to find some way that people from a variety of cultures could share their understanding of what the moral life is. As I looked for a moral theology that helped my neighbor in Rome or in New York, I also wanted something that could guide my own life. In my quest, I discovered the virtues. Aquinas' work on them offered exactly what I had wanted, a moral theology for ordinary living that encompassed every human action and urged readers to attain the *ends* of specific virtues by practicing them as *means*. Moral theology built upon the virtues helps the church express the Gospels while being attuned to the ordinariness of everyday life.

Imaginative Students Use the Virtues

After I became a teacher, I found confirmation of virtue ethics among my own students. Doctoral students at Fordham University imaginatively applied the virtues to a variety of contexts.

A mother of four college students wrote on prudence, Aquinas, and motherhood. Now a professor at St. John's University, she described how Aquinas' understanding of prudence is similar to the practical reasoning proposed by today's feminists. A Long Island diocesan priest studied the American Bishops' economic pastoral and proposed that the document would have been more successful had it used ordinary virtue language rather than technical, academic principles: in that way, preachers could have used the document to make the insights of justice more evident and alive for their congregations. A woman now teaching at Florida's Barry University wrote on self-determination and Aquinas's virtues. A Mennonite minister noted the compatibility of virtue ethics for Christian spirituality. A Greek Orthodox priest wrote on the importance of virtue for the Orthodox communion.

Today, at Weston Jesuit School of Theology, I teach a Marist priest who studies what virtue offers to emerging democracies as they seek concrete goals for a responsible citizenry. He will eventually return to his native Tonga where an absolute monarch rules. An Irish Jesuit prepares for his future work in spiritual direction by writing on friendship in the writings of Saint Aelred. An Australian diocesan priest finishes his licentiate (STL) thesis on the historical relationship between shame and the returning warrior and now begins his STD (Weston's first in fifty years!) to study prudence and self-deception. An American woman lawyer studies depression and moral reasoning, while a South African woman business executive studies the virtues and accounting. As I write this essay, a Ph.d. candidate from Ottawa has called with a proposal on prudence and fatherhood, and another from Boston College drafts his proposal on reconciliation and hospitality.

This survey illustrates the promise of moral theology. It stands as a refreshing reminder that the Catholic tradition is richer than many of the current debates, for we Catholics can get caught up with particular issues and lose sight of the bigger picture. Seeing that picture, imaginatively, helps us overcome divisiveness.

The agenda of moral theology is expanded by using the virtues, which envelope the fullness of human life. The virtues speak to a variety of cultures, while providing a context for that dialogue. For example, although patience might not look the same in Los Angeles as it does in Biloxi or Madrid, it is still patience, a virtue identifiable in most cultures. Likewise the virtues are found in a variety of religious cultures, not only in Christian ones, but also in Eastern, African, and Mediterranean culture. While the virtues expand our ability to think of the moral life, they extend our horizons beyond borders and religions; they enlarge our ability to communicate.

Using the Virtues in the Parish

For Catholics the virtues provide an extraordinary opportunity to apply our tradition to the concrete life of the parish. I offer here three suggestions.

1. Preaching. Taking the words and deeds of Jesus and explaining them is much easier than applying them to ordinary life. The virtues provide an embodied context to flesh out that application. We preachers can draw analogies, for instance, between prudence as we know it and the prudence of the five virgins (or of the imprudence of the man with the one talent). We can talk about the hope that animates Zaccheus as he climbs the tree, the charity that prompts the widow to give her entire savings or the faith of the Centurion who sought healing for his daughter. But we can also use these insights as points of departure, asking "What does faith really mean today for the believer? Is hope the same for a first-century Jew as for a twentieth-century Philadelphian?"

The virtues should be brought into contemporary life; they are, after all, designed for the concrete. We can preach the virtue of biblical figures and also demonstrate how that virtue is lived out in the lives of the parishioners. The generous and forgiving spirit of the prodigal's father, for example, not only conveys the extraordinary bounteousness of our God, but occasions a moment of reflection on the reconciling spirit of our particular parish. From the preacher's mouth, the virtues become conduits between the Word Made Flesh and hearers of that Word.

2. Parish Education. Parishioners often wonder whether their convictions are deep enough, whether when they are concerned for themselves, whether they are being selfish or self-caring, and whether they properly understand justice and equality or fidelity and love. Parishioners also look to see whether the tradition is resourceful enough to guide them in the affairs of daily life.

They know that Augustine, Aquinas, and others are important figures in the tradition but they may not know that the main contribution to the moral life made by these saints was their writings on the virtues. Many parishioners are concerned with their families, for which the virtues are particularly important. What, for example, does prudence look like for a mother, a father, a teenager? What does fidelity look like for a youngster, a spouse, an in-law? When should a parent turn to self-care? What do bravery and temperance mean in the lives of young adults? As rich traditional resources designed to help church members with practical life, the virtues can well be adopted for parish educational programs.

3. Parish Identity and Goals. Parish communities are constantly examining themselves and establishing priorities. Virtue ethics can help. As a parish begins to plan, it can assess itself in terms of the virtues: Does it possess the quality of mercy? Is it a center of justice and is it identifiable for its fidelity? Do prudence, humility, and a reconciling spirit animate the parish council and advisors? Does hospitality animate those who first meet people calling at the parish center or rectory? Are the pastor and staff known to be wise, generous, faithful, and brave?

As parish leaders set parish goals, they can also engage the virtues. The virtues, always concerned about ends, express not only the people we are but the people we can become. By practicing the virtues, parishes do become more virtuous, overcoming vices such as mean-spiritedness, narrowness, and faint-heartedness. The virtues, then, become the conduits for the parish's self-understanding, growth, and greater service.

Just as my students continue to push forward the agenda of the virtues by exploring areas to which they can be applied, so parish leaders can use the virtues to assist the parish in realizing its mission. It is, after all, the legacy of virtue to ask the twofold question: Who are we? And who are we called to become? Answering it is always an imaginative and prudential agenda.

Questions for Reflection

1. Name several practices or exercises that you perform to grow in fidelity, e.g., to contact friends on a regular basis.

____

____

____

____

2. Name several practices or exercises that you perform to grow in justice, e.g., to join Amnesty International and support the rights of prisoners of conscience.

____

____

____

____

3. What is your opinion of self-care as a cardinal virtue?

____

____

____

____

4. Recount two instances when justice and fidelity recently conflicted.

____

____

____

____

5. Were these conflicts prudentially resolved?

____

____

____

____

6. Do you think that self-care should ever override concerns of justice and/ or fidelity?

____

____

____

____

7. How would you teach a younger person the virtue of courage?

____

____

____

____

8. How would you teach a younger person the virtue of temperance?

____

____

____

____

9. Do you feel that the virtues help you to set an agenda for your life?

____

____

____

____

Part IV

Other Virtues

Introduction

IN THIS PART, I OFFER DESCRIPTIONS OF SEVERAL IMPORTANT virtues important for Christians. This is not meant to be a complete list; on the contrary, it is meant to generate in readers the desire to discuss other virtues as well. Though the cardinal virtues describe the fundamental virtues necessary for the upright person, these virtues in this part highlight the fact that the virtuous life is not so much the life we live as the life we aim at. If growing in the service of charity is the Christian challenge, then the virtues are the stuff that we should practice in order to realize that charity. Our imaginations should help us see the virtues not as another set of duties, but rather as a new opportunity to strive to become fully alive human beings.

❋

SIXTEEN

Hospitality

WHAT IS THE WORST SERMON YOU EVER HEARD? PERHAPS there were several and, if so, one of them had to be about Martha and Mary. No gospel story has generated more sanctimonious sermons than that one. For centuries, people in the pews have had to listen to self-serving messages in which preachers insisted that Jesus was commending the spiritual life over the practical life. The contemplative life of scholarship and prayer was a greater vocation, they contended, than the work in a soup-kitchen or by a common-laborer. Karl Rahner was according to this distinction more important than Dorothy Day.

I always thought the distinction was false and I thought that we should not accept its claim. These sentiments were not only shared by me, but by many. A good friend of mine, a Basque Jesuit brother living in Rome thought the distinction ridiculous. With a bit of irony, he would introduce himself saying, "I am Jose Luis Ruiz. As a Jesuit brother I belong to the Society of St. Martha. We work very hard because in the Jesuits with so many priests, there are so many Marys." As the son of a cop and a secretary, I shared his sympathies. I could not believe that Jesus would recommend the sedentary academic over the industrious worker.

Yet, I could not deny that in the Gospels Jesus corrected Martha and praised Mary. But, why? Only recently I heard a new explanation of the story from a wonderful Jesuit, Howard Gray. Remember what's going on in the story? Jesus is visiting his friends. Mary has been sitting with Jesus in (let's call it) the living room and from the kitchen (why not?) we hear Martha's grumbling and anger rising. Noise continues until finally Martha comes out and tries to drag Jesus into her squabble with Mary. Imagine what the guest, Jesus, feels like.

We can, because, unfortunately, we too have been caught in scenes like that. Invited to a couple's house, we become aware shortly after arriving that one of our hosts is distracted about something. As time goes on, we realize that one host is annoyed at the other. The angry host, who has hardly said a polite, let alone a hospitable word, has been making all sorts of under-his-breath comments. Finally, he launches into a moody tirade about his spouse not helping him. Lovely. Nothing is more unpleasant. And now we are angry: though we might feel that the spouse is indeed never helpful in the kitchen, we have no sympathy today for our thoughtless host. As a guest, we are in a vulnerable position; we think that no guest should be so treated.

Jesus' words then about Martha and Mary are not about each choosing a different vocation. Rather, since they both invited Jesus, both should be hospitable, but only one lets him feel that he is a guest. Jesus' admonition is strong; he wants Martha to see the worthiness of her original intention.

Hospitality: the Divine Virtue

Hospitality is the virtue that God practices. Wherever God is in the Scriptures (excepting perhaps the exile and the flood), God is hospitable. Right from the beginning of the Scriptures, we see the Creator fashioning the world and placing us into the Garden where we have everything we will ever need. In God's creation, God is eminently hospitable.

Though we are exiled by our own disobedience, we are fashioned clothing for our journey. But, even in the exile, God's hospitality touches us in the land and food provided. And even when we kill our own brother, God marks us and protects us in this world that God has made.

The Israelites knew well of God's hospitality, which brought them out of slavery and into the land of milk and honey. Thus they were called to be hospitable to the stranger, and so their father Abraham was hospitable to the angels; while those in Sodom violated them. The God who gives us our place, the God who makes us stranger no longer is the same God who demands that we too be hospitable to the stranger.

Jesus as the Paradigm of Hospitality

The life of Jesus is the story of the one who became flesh for us but whom we, in turn, did not welcome but rather crucified. Right from the beginning of his life, Jesus finds the world inhospitable. In Matthew's gospel, Jesus must be taken from the land that was given his forebearers and return to the land of slavery for the sake of sanctuary. In Luke, his parents are refused human shelter, and Jesus is born homeless. The homelessness of Jesus is emphasized when his first visitors come and they like him live without shelter. And even when he matures, though he is at first welcomed into the temple, he is quickly taken to be thrown from the cliffs of his own native place.

In some key exchanges with his disciples, Jesus instructs them in hospitality. He multiplies the loaves and fishes precisely when his disciples try to send his listeners away. When the twelve try to keep away children, Jesus admonishes them again. Similarly, anyone who extends to him an invitation, he accepts, whether tax collector, Pharisee, or friend. Likewise his parables often focus on hospitality (and its lack) whether they are about a wounded man, an abandoned father, or a wealthy landlord. Finally, his depiction of the last judgment is based nearly exclusively on hospitableness: feeding the hungry, clothing the naked, welcoming the stranger.

As he approaches his death, Jesus is heroically hospitable. The foretelling of his death is frequently tied to his intention to prepare the way for us so that we may be in his Father's house. At the last supper, which he has longed to celebrate with the twelve, Jesus becomes the quintessential host, washing their feet and instructing them to do as he does. (Foot-washing is not simply confined to the upper room. Precisely at the house of Simon a woman washes Jesus' feet with her tears. When Simon tries to admonish both Jesus and the woman, Jesus praises her for her hospitality and reprimands Simon for his lack of it.)

On the cross, his concern for hospitality peaks. Jesus turns to his disciple John and to his mother Mary and offers them to one another and directs that they care for one another. Then he speaks with the good thief and offers him that day a place in his Father's house. Finally, in preparing the way for us, he petitions our pardon from God.

The Lesson of Hospitality

Surely we are struck at how apparent the virtue of hospitality is in the Scriptures and how often we miss it. Consider the story of Martha and Mary, a story about hospitality that for centuries became known as the tale of two vocations. We missed what Jesus is teaching us which is to be hospitable, as he and his Father are hospitable.

Why is hospitality so important? Hospitality is important because it recognizes the vulnerable state of the stranger. When we are hospitable we recognize that our guest does not now have precisely what we can offer her: a home, a roof, a room, a bed, that is, a place of her own.

We can also offer her companionship, human company, a community, precisely what she as stranger does not have. What we have is precisely what she does not.

Of course, what we have is itself a gift. We have a place of our own and human companionship because we have been given them; we too can easily find ourselves without either. Hospitality is then the recognition of what we have as gift and what we can give as gift.

But hospitality is above all human attentiveness. The stranger, like the wounded man on the road to Jericho or the prodigal son on the pig farm, is stranger to the extent that he is ignored. Nothing is more degrading than to be ignored. Recall, for instance, the contemporary, and unfortunately familiar and frequent, complaint of so many homeless people begging, "People pass me as if I am not here."

Jesus was ignored by Martha, the wounded man by the priest and scribe, the prodigal son by his brother. A human can never be more abjectly treated than to be ignored. It was for this reason that bleeding Lazarus at the gate was welcomed into the bosom of Abraham and the rich man was not.

Like those in the Last Judgment, the rich man is punished for ignoring those in need. From the viewpoint of God as our judge, then, nothing can be more harmful to us than to ignore another.

There are then three reasons for being hospitable: because God is and has been hospitable to us; because the stranger requires it; and because God commands it. If hospitality were simply a duty, these three reasons would be sufficient. But, hospitality is not simply a duty but a virtue. Unlike a duty, virtue is its own reward.

Here then we see that we are commanded to be hospitable not only for the good of the stranger, but also for our own good. Indeed, here we better understand, I think, the Mary and Martha story. Jesus admonishes Martha not because she fails at being a dutiful host, but because she misses out on the pleasure of being a host and of enjoying her guest.

Many of us can be dutiful hosts. But we know the difference between hosting as a duty and hosting as a pleasure. Only the latter benefits both host and guest.

From the moment God breathed into us in the Garden, from that moment until now God has been teaching us the virtue of hospitality, for God has been attentive to us, and we believe that God does this because it is God's pleasure. Knowing our vulnerabilities and knowing what we lack, God has been providential. God calls us likewise to the divine practice of attending to humanity. Nothing can elevate us more, both when we practice it and when we receive it. And nothing can bring us more pleasure, if only we let it.

✵

SEVENTEEN

Wisdom

"KEENAN? THIS IS FUCHS. HOW WAS YOUR FLIGHT? GOOD? Fine. You will have supper in my community tonight. Is that all right? Fine. And then we will go out beer drinking. Is that all right? Good. Welcome to Rome." I had met Josef Fuchs the previous summer, in 1981, when while studying Italian in Florence I went to Rome to see whether I could do a dissertation there. I had written to him and he was pleasant and receptive enough. Now, a year later, I had been ordained, finished my degree at Weston and had only arrived an hour earlier when Fuchs called. It was the first day of five years of study in Rome.

I had dinner with him that night. "Would you mind proofing the copies of my latest book with Georgetown Press. You don't have classes for another month and I need an American who can check for spelling and punctuation mistakes." "Sure," I said.

I was petrified. Here was Josef Fuchs who at 70 years of age was probably the greatest Catholic moral theologian of the twentieth century. He had written his dissertation on the identity of the Church as priest, prophet and king and two books, one on the sexual ethics of Thomas Aquinas and another on natural law. Then he took to writing essays in the Jesuit journal *Stimmen der Zeit*, (*The Signs of the Times*). He had written an article on every major topic in my field.

Over eighty of his essays would be translated into English alone. And he wanted me to proof his texts. I did.

I remember my first exam with him. At the Gregorian University in Rome, we had to take eighteen courses in preparation for the doctorate and usually the grade for each course was determined by a simple ten minute oral exam. With some classes having up to two hundred students in them, these exams though brief for us were interminable for the professors. So, I would arrive for each exam with a list of the readings I had done for the course. The professors always picked up on my offer and asked questions based on the list I submitted. To Fuchs I gave a list of articles on the Church's authority, in particular, the original writings of those who drafted the Church's documents on its teaching authority at both Vatican I and Vatican II. Fuchs asked me questions; I answered. "Cardinal Ratzinger does not hold that interpretation," he said. "I know, but this is what the Council fathers decided." "Perhaps, but Cardinal Ratzinger decides today." "But . . ." "Never mind, your exam is over." Out I went.

Fuchs had reason to understand authority. From at least Trent, and some may argue before that, the moral theologian's basic work was to decide what was right and what was wrong, to determine it and to publish it in a series of books or manuals for priests to read. Then, annually national groups of moral theologians would get together and discuss any issue that needed discussion. The story goes that in the mid-sixties in the United States the moral theologians got together to discuss all sorts of topics. One topic was birth control. Each moralist said it was always wrong to directly intend artificial birth control. Except the last person, who remarked, "I heard Fuchs has changed his opinion." They went around the room again and several moralists changed their positions.

Fuchs indeed changed his position. Early in Vatican II, Pope John XXIII established a committee of bishops and cardinals, theologians and lay people to study the teaching on birth control. As they worked, it became clear to many members that the papal teaching for the past eighty years should be changed. After his own election, Pope Paul VI, perhaps concerned that the committee was too progressive put more conservative bishops and theologians on the committee. Fuchs, a well-respected conservative Roman theologian and an opponent to artificial birth control, was among the new appointees. On the committee, however, he began to hear testimony by a variety of lay people about their experiences with rhythm and birth control. More importantly, he began to listen to lay people and the way they reasoned.

On the committee Fuchs' real conversion was not that he went from thinking birth control was wrong to thinking that it was right. (He didn't; to my knowledge he never claimed that birth control was right). Rather, he realized that because it is such a serious matter, married couples had to work out in their consciences, informed by the Scriptures and Church teaching, what they should do regarding birth control. Fuchs' conversion was that he no longer saw the moral theologian as the final decision-maker of what is right or wrong; rather, he claimed that the most competent person to make a serious decision is the one who has to act.

Fuchs was converted by listening. He subsequently authored the (nearly complete) majority position of the committee. Of course the rest is history. The small minority argued that the papacy should not change Church teaching. On this premise Pope Paul VI thanked the committee for its work, distanced himself from the majority position and issued the very different *Humanae vitae.*

In changing his position, Fuchs changed his vocation. Now he would no longer be the final decision-maker; now, he wanted to train future moral theologians who could sensitively assist people in making right decisions. So much so, he stressed that if I wanted to be a good moralist, I had to hear confessions, preach at mass, listen to the people's comments, and find out what the people thought. "If you don't do pastoral work, you won't be a good moralist."

Every summer, Fuchs would leave Rome and go off to do the same in a parish in either Austria or Germany. Since I used my summers to study German, I tagged along to wherever he went. (Once he forgot that he had told me that we were going to Cologne and at the last minute he went to Vienna. I lived in Cologne, with people constantly asking me "Tell me again why you're in Cologne?") Fuchs would live in a parish, I in a neighboring Jesuit community. I would meet up with him once a week, when he would take me to see a neighboring city.

In visiting a famous town or city I have the custom of paying respects to its population by visiting a famous townsperson's grave, birthplace, or workplace. One day we went to Salzburg. He wanted to show me the Baroque Churches and to take me to his favorite restaurant. "The last time I ate there, I ate with Kohlberg. We were here at a conference on conscience. I kept asking him, 'Lawrence, what do you mean by conscience?' He couldn't answer me."

While in Salzburg with Fuchs, I told him that I wanted to find Mozart's birthplace. He said, "You know, I have never been there either; we'll find it after lunch." We got to his restaurant; it looked like a house. We went up a long staircase, passing rooms that looked like they belonged to a museum. We kept climbing till Fuchs said, "Ah, here we are." We sat down; ordered two schnapps, and looked at the menu. "Josef, do you know the name of this place?" "You know, I don't. I have eaten here for years; I don't know the name." "It's Mozart's birthplace." We laughed.

As outgoing as he is, Fuchs is silent about many things. A few years ago, he wrote "Occasionally I have said: I do not say anything I do not stand behind, but maybe I do not say everything behind which I stand. I think it is generally wrong to want to provoke. In the face of possible difficulties from the magisterium a person must get a sense of what may be said under the circumstances, what must be said, and what should not be said."

One topic that he never talks about is what happened on the birth control commission. "I took an oath not to report anything from there." "But others have spoken," I added, telling him that my understanding of the committee was from books that I read. "I know those authors; they wanted me to speak; they spoke like you, 'others have spoken.' " "How did you answer?" "I told them: 'I took an oath; if others speak, that's for their conscience, but I took an oath." Here was the man that others had (wrongly) branded as the great consequentialist.

Now in his mid-eighties, Fuchs still writes regularly in *Stimmen der Zeit*. As any theologian knows, he has changed the face of moral theology. But I think if he were to single out his proudest moment it may be this one: During the years of the student rebellions, the Gregorian's student body was noticeably tame. Still, in the early seventies there was some student unrest and the old Jesuit fathers at the Gregorian didn't know what to do. The dean asked Fuchs to meet with the students. "They wanted a few things; they were reasonable."

* * *

Wisdom has a very human face. For me, Josef Fuchs is one embodiment of wisdom. But each of us can tell stories of a wise advisor, parent, or friend. Whoever they are, I would suggest that they have the following traits in common. First, wisdom is personable. I know that we think of the genius as tortured, like Ezra Pound, but my experience of the wise person is that she is personable. For every odd genius, there are an equal number of affable wise people. Second, wisdom is engaging. That is why the Word became flesh. Third, human wisdom is hospitable. It never intimidates. (I always know that whenever someone described to me as "bright" acts condescendingly that he is certainly not secure with his "wisdom.") True wisdom does not lord it over others. Fourth, wisdom is open and seeks to understand better whatever is necessary to get things right. Fifth, wisdom is ongoing. Any wise person is continually examining her thought, as critical of herself as she is of anyone. Wisdom is something in which we grow. Sixth, human wisdom errs. Fuchs' conversion was not simply a change; he recognized that he should have been listening to others' consciences. Admitting error is the true sign of wisdom. Seventh, the wise "believer" loves the Church. One cannot be wise in the Church and not love it. Eighth, the wise person has integrity and especially does not compromise her beliefs or her conscience. Ninth, the wise person recognizes authority and respects it. Otherwise, one thinks oneself alone is the only authority. Tenth, true wisdom is practical; it serves others. It has human purpose. Eleventh, the wise person is able to laugh at himself, to recognize his limits, to recognize his humanity. Twelfth, true wisdom respects others. I remember, vividly, my first day in Rome, not only Fuchs' offer but the repetition of the phrase, "Is that alright with you." It is the constant question of someone who can wisely advise. Finally, true wisdom delights in the truth, which is not some utterance, but as Karl Rahner once wrote, "profoundly personal." That is why the wise person loves.

✵

EIGHTEEN

Gratitude

IN HIS WONDERFUL *THE ONCE AND FUTURE KING*, T. H. WHITE described the creation. If my memory serves me right, it goes like this. . . . God had finished creating the world, the seas, the heavens, the plants and had just finished with the animals, when God decided to give the animals a special role in the creation. God called all the animal embryos together and told them that each species could ask for one "improvement." So the first one asked to be able to forage where others couldn't; so God gave the aardvark embryo a snout so long that it wouldn't even have to dig its way into furrows. Another embryo was concerned that there were too many animals and not enough food. It asked to be able to eat leaves where other animals couldn't and so God gave the giraffe embryo long legs and a long neck to eat the tops of trees. Another said it was afraid of being attacked. It didn't want to be mixed up with the smelly skunk so it asked if God could provide some last minute protection and God gave the porcupine quills that could radiate out at will. One after another, each embryo had a request: the bat wanted special hearing, the panther wanted to be quick, and the lion wanted to be king of the jungle. Finally there was the human. God asked it, "what do you want?" The human responded, "I was thinking; you're God and it looks like you have already done a lot of work. And I can't think of what else I need. So I figure, if I need it you'll give it to me; otherwise, I just want to thank you for all the work." God was very pleased with the human. God said, "Human you are my greatest creation; yet you will be born without any special improvements: you will have no wings like the birds, no speed like the cats, no strength like the great beasts, no protection like the armadillos or the rhinoceros. You will look like an embryo in the womb, at birth, and throughout life; you will be completely vulnerable, but you will be wise, because you are." And the human embryo said "thanks," and went off with the rest of the embryos waiting to be born.

Misery

Despite the sense of well-being we enjoy when we are grateful, often we are not. For instance, when I'm tired, my dark side tends to come out and I'm not that resistant to it. When it emerges, it spawns self-pity, anger, and righteousness along with it. I forget how happy my life is and how I got to be happy. Instead, I think that the little I have, I am entitled to and should have more. I believe that I am completely self-made and pretty faultless. I think I am the only one who works and the only one whose work is credible. I become self-absorbed and terribly condescending. I measure not myself, but others and I look only to put down those around me. I look at what they do and utter a snide, dismissive remark about them and their work. I am presumptuous about myself. I look at my life with smugness and resist anyone who tries to tell me that I may be a little severe or, God forbid, defensive. And as I hurt others, I hurt myself, painting myself into a corner of nastiness.

Not everyone's dark side is like that. While mine is aggressive and sarcastic, others have a rather passive dark side. They may just be silent and moody. Others may capitalize on the moodiness and use it to manipulate others to do things the way they want it. Others simply whine.

Whiners blame others for not helping them more, for not being there more, for not giving them more credit, for not appreciating them more. In a word, they whine because they want people to dote on them, even adore them. Whiners are especially hard on their parents. And some whiners continue their whining about their parents even as adults.

I believe that anyone can whine about their parents until they are thirty. After that, they should stop (unless they never did before and their therapist insists on it)! Ten or fifteen years of blaming parents is awfully vicious to parents, but it is also vicious to the whiner. To be over thirty and to continue whining about one's parents is to continue to see oneself as a child. Such behavior is simply self-indulgence. And to blame others at that stage, ignores the real issue: by thirty we should have begun to live our own lives.

Whether our dark side is aggressive or passive, when it dominates, we are miserable. And when we are miserable we are as vicious to others as we are to ourselves. For just as virtuous activity enhances others and in particular the acting person, so too vicious activity harms others and, in particular, the acting person.

Instead of whining or dominating, being grateful is the disposition of really sitting back and looking at all the gifts we have. Gratitude helps us to see where we are in our lives, not as we stretch forward, but rather as others have extended themselves to us.

We have real gratitude when we exercise our memory. But we must exercise our memories when we are happy. A miserable person has miserable memories. (As Aristotle said, we see things the way we are!) If we are happy and we look back at our lives with happiness we remember the ways that people helped shape our lives so well.

Memory is the most affective dimension of all our thought processes. No other thinking activity is as filled with images, persons, relationships, or feelings. The Italians know this; their word for the verb to remember is *ricordare,* to bring back to the heart. If the heart is happy, it recollects events, occasions, loves as gifts.

But people are happy because they are grateful. Grateful memories nurture the happy spirit and uplift the heart. The virtue of gratitude sustains and furthers the better disposition of the human being.

A Paradox

The difficulty with developing gratitude, however, is that those who most need it are precisely those least able to acquire it. The miserable person only brings resentment back to the heart. Feeding resentful images to an already miserable heart only leaves it more bitter. And since memory is so affective, the memories themselves become oppressive burdens. How then does the miserable person ever become happy? If memories are the stuff of gratitude how can they be recalled happily by the unhappy person?

Satisfaction

The key to acquiring gratitude is satisfaction. The human embryo's decision to voice its satisfaction with God's creation gave it a spirit of gratitude. Had the human spent its time thinking about longer arms, thicker skin, or stronger heels it would never have seen all that it already had. Seeing what it had, and being satisfied with its lot, it was able to enjoy. (Of course, the irony of the fall then was that eating the fruit is not simply an act of disobedience, but an act of ingratitude. No longer being satisfied, the human lost gratitude and wanted more wisdom, precisely when human wisdom was greatest, as White suggests, in its satisfaction!)

Gratitude can enter into the dry spirits of an unhappy person who suspends for a moment his misery and looks at his lot with a desire not for what is missing, but a sense of quiet satisfaction with where one is.

Satisfaction is not some passive state. Satisfaction does not mean that one should resign oneself to being poor, alone, downcast, etc. Rather satisfaction is dynamic: it is the act of informing the heart, that one's lot could be a lot worse, that one has been helped, that even in loneliness there has been, as Williams reminds us, the kindness of strangers. Satisfaction is the act of harnessing in the whining or of subduing the defensive haughtiness. Satisfaction curbs the melancholic and the condescending.

The chronically miserable person is that way when he is not satisfied. He forgets that misery does not come out of nowhere. Rather its festering, parasitic way is sustained and cultivated by the human person. Satisfaction on the other hand prompts the miserable person to drop the defensiveness and/or indulgence. Satisfaction urges the person to reexamine the state of his situation, and to try to see whether, anywhere, there has been a moment of gift, caring or support.

As I get older I depend more and more on satisfaction and gratitude. I know that my dark demanding side is never tempered but by satisfaction. And I know my memories are always pathetically vicious when I am miserable. But I've learned more and more that my happiness is dependent on my gratitude and my gratitude is dependent upon satisfaction. I can always tell how happy I am by how grateful I am; whenever I find myself spontaneously grateful, I know how well things are going in my life.

As I've grown in satisfaction, I have tried remembering more of my past: my family, my neighbors, my formation in the Society of Jesus, my colleagues. In that satisfaction, I have discovered how terribly narrow and selective my memory was when I was more miserable. I've learned instead that satisfaction and then gratitude has wide and extensive memories.

For instance, I remember when after five years of studies in Rome, how my folks met me at the airport. They were driving me from Kennedy Airport to Fordham University where I would begin teaching in only five days. We stopped at a restaurant for lunch. I told them that day: "I'm very happy to be back so that I can tell you how grateful I am for all you've given and continue to give to me." I was surprised how there was nothing at all manufactured in those long sought after words. They flowed naturally and brought happiness to them and to me. The words were more a part of me than my own more constructed misery. And when I said those words I realized how true they were: I was really fortunate to have these two wonderful people as my parents.

Those words, I have since learned again and again, are crucial for every relationship I have. They are not often spoken, but when they are I realize how blest I am. As I learn to leave an occasionally miserable disposition behind, they have become for me the most important words in my life.

✵

NINETEEN

Sympathy

THE TRUE SIGN OF VIRTUE, WE HAVE KNOWN SINCE ARISTOTLE, is that it is never excessive: neither too much nor too little. Another expression is that virtue is the mean between extremes. The simplest expression is then "Virtue is the mean." No virtue needs to observe the mean more than sympathy: too little sympathy is clearly a vice; but so too is too much sympathy.

Too much Sympathy?

What do I mean by too much sympathy? Anyone who has lost a loved one has encountered too much sympathy. For instance, finally being able to return to work, the grieving person recognizes that her colleagues appreciate what she has been through. By returning to work, the person also finds some security. In the aftermath of the upheaval that follows any death, a return to the routine of work provides a basis of stability not found in a grieving household. For a grieving person, the workplace is often a sanctuary, an oasis.

In an odd sort of way, while the returning colleague wants the distracting activity of work, she also appreciates her colleagues' ability to know that some days she will function well and some days, not so well. She will appreciate kind condolences and simple, gracious signs of sympathy. But as she tries awkwardly to renegotiate her life, the last thing she wants is to be trapped by a sympathizing colleague who insists on asking her in front of everyone else, "How are you? No, really how are you? Are you all right?"

These albeit honest expressions of concern are not a help. The expression of sympathy is to be attentive to the feelings of the person in need. When we place the person in need in an embarrassing situation we are not showing them sympathy; we are adding to their awkwardness because we are not attentive to their feelings.

It is like the person who insists that every grieving person wants to talk and so asks one agonizing question after another. Or the one who insists that the person should talk when she just wants to take things quietly in stride.

Perhaps the oddest expressions of sympathy transpire at wakes. So many people attentive to the grieving family's feelings know that there are only a few words that make any sense; they know that being there is more important than saying the perfect phrase. Yet others insist that they know exactly what should be said. They toss out some phrases like "you just have to accept God's will" or "maybe it is just as well." These expressions are spoken when the speaker simply believes that everyone grieves in the same way. They repeat the same phrases elsewhere. They are professional mourners.

Too much sympathy comes from people who never pay attention to the feelings of the person in need. Rather than measuring what's right by the person who is in need, they consider what they would want or what they think would be appropriate for themselves. In a manner of speaking, they are condescending, believing only what they think or feel is the norm. But the notion of sympathy is, as Adam Smith called it, "fellow-feeling," feeling what the other feels. To be sympathetic is to try to enter into what the other feels: the sympathetic response is the one then that simply tries to resonate with another.

Too Little Sympathy?

The clearest sign of too little sympathy is found regularly on the streets of America in the way we pass the homeless. Certainly there are many times that facing the homeless on our streets, we are at a loss to know what we should do. On the one hand, there are many homeless whom we often meet asking us for financial help. On the other hand, many people who serve the homeless say that we should not give to individuals but rather to organizations that serve the homeless. So we usually do not give anything and instead we often simply wish that they weren't there. They are a problem; we want them to go away.

The attention in all this is not on the homeless person; rather it is on ourselves. The discomfort is not what the homeless person feels; it's what we feel. So we ignore the homeless. And a homeless person knows it. Her most common complaint is, "he acts as if he doesn't even see me."

But the momentary discomfort we feel is perhaps an opportunity to feel their discomfort. We may rightly decide not to give them some financial assistance (hopefully we do provide something to the agencies), but we may at least greet them, recognize them, share our humanity with them, simply by acknowledging them.

Our resistance to sympathy appears often enough in the way we look at people from other lands. Though we are an extraordinarily generous country we act sometimes like the overtaxed eldest sibling who reacts to a family member's loss as "his" problem. Before feeling the least sense of sympathy for the family member who is suffering, he only thinks that whatever the suffering, it will simply be transferred to his already burdened shoulders. Like him (I am one), we are absorbed in our own feelings, our own discomfort, without any attentiveness to these other people whose own feelings are overwhelmed.

So often our reaction to other people's difficulties looks like it comes right out of a "I'm-not-co-dependent-anymore" manual. So worried about whether we are going to feel compelled to respond to another nation's "hard-luck story," we are more interested in extricating ourselves from any involvement than simply acknowledging their own situation. We arm ourselves against feeling any sympathy by uttering such hapless expressions as "They should take care of themselves." Worse, we pit people living in poverty in our own nation against those suffering elsewhere: "We have our own to take care of." The phrase is riddled with contradictions, but above all it keeps us from feeling anything.

Through a variety of rhetorical phrases we distance ourselves from any feeling for another. We manage to isolate our feelings, our perceptions, our senses. We do not want to feel what they are feeling.

I think we engineer our feelings for others in need precisely because by nature all human beings have a disposition for sympathy. It is why we tear when others do. So, in order to not feel sympathy, we try to distance ourselves from having any feeling. We are afraid of the consequences: if we feel for them, next we will have to do something for them.

True sympathy is simply feeling with another. It is not necessarily doing something; whether we should do something belongs to justice, fidelity and self-care. But sympathy is simply allowing ourselves to feel naturally for another in need. Sympathy is appreciating another's plight.

As a feeling it is prior to any decision about action. It is simply the ability to resonate with another; to recognize her situation as it is. When we are sympathetic we let another's situation enter into our own blood stream. We drop any acquired defenses. Rather we allow ourselves to feel (naturally, spontaneously) what any normal human feels when encountering another in need.

Professionalism warns us against getting too involved in the lives of too many. Co-dependency groups warn us rightly against responding to another in need simply in order to answer our own compulsive need of needing to be needed. Both of these are important correctives. They lead us away from overacting.

But sympathy is not about acting. It's just about feeling. To be sympathetic simply means that we can feel somehow what another does. That's not co-dependency; on the contrary, the problem with co-dependency is that one is trapped by one's own need to be needed. But by sympathy we can feel the other's suffering. We may not be able to answer their suffering or perhaps for some reason we should not be the ones to respond to their suffering. In either event, what we should do is subsequent to what we do feel. Sympathy is first registering that another is suffering and then letting that person's feeling enter into us.

After my brother's death and then my Dad's I learned a simple mantra. "You can't feel the good feelings if you don't feel the bad." I realized that if I didn't feel the sorrow of their deaths, if I did not face the loss, if I didn't let go of all my devices of control and fall into the terrible feelings of grief, I would never know a happy memory, a consoling grace, a grateful recollection, a profound hope. If I shut off one set of feelings, all of the rest would be lost.

The same works for sympathy. Arresting sympathy harms not only the one in need but the one who resists sympathy. A cold person never feels sympathy, nor does she feel joy. A warm person feels the pain of another and their joy as well. There is no cost to our sympathy. It's only what we feel naturally. If we lose it, we lose our humanity.

✵

TWENTY

Humor

THIS GUY GOES UP TO A DOMINICAN PRIEST AND ASKS "Can I do a novena in order to win a Lexus?" "What's a Lexus?," asks the Dominican. "It's the 'state-of-the-art' car. It's the dream car of so many." "You want to do a novena for a *car*! No, you can't do a novena for a car." A few days later the guy goes up to a Benedictine and asks "Can I do a novena in order to win a Lexus?" "What's a Lexus?," asks the Benedictine. "It's the car Clinton refused to let into the country in his trade war with Japan. It's a wonderful car." "You want to do a novena for a *car*! No, you can't." Finally a week later the guy finds a Jesuit and asks "Can I do a novena in order to win a Lexus?" "What's a novena?," asks the Jesuit.

Humor is based on a target; no target, no humor. Of course, if humor is a virtue, it observes the mean. If we target someone repeatedly or excessively, the humor is no longer virtuous; it's only an excuse to harm someone. But humor is a virtue; it belongs to human flourishing.

I love humor. I love being with people who make me laugh; it is for me a sign of life, of intelligence, of joy. Good humor, clever humor targets its own members. I love being with friends or family members willing to target themselves or the ones they are with, rather than someone else. I love when I can laugh at myself (that isn't always);

I love when I can laugh at my friends. When I laugh at myself or at my friends, I am at home with my humanity.

Humor and Human Vulnerability

We humans are vulnerable. We are thin skinned. We use a variety of devices to protect ourselves, to keep ourselves from being hurt, bothered, disturbed, shaken. But when we laugh at ourselves, we are at home with ourselves and with those with whom we laugh. And together, we are at home being vulnerable human beings.

In my family, my brother is able to get us all laughing. We can always tell Sean stories. My favorite is when he made his first confession. Sean walked into the confessional, said his sins and left. About two months later, he returned to the confessional, entered, began confessing his sins, when suddenly he heard the priest's panel slide and heard a voice say, "What's your rush, son? I didn't hear what you were saying." Sean nearly fell out of the confessional. He never knew that there was supposed to be a priest listening. For his first confession the priest was listening to the person on the other side; for his second, a penitent was finishing up on the other side and when the person finished, the priest slid open the screen, catching my brother's confession half way through.

Sean told us the story. Sean is not afraid of telling us funny stories. He's at home with his humanity. I love being with him; he makes me feel at ease with myself as well.

We are, however, not always virtuous when we laugh at ourselves. Sometimes its just a veneer; sometimes it's a sign that we have no self-respect; sometimes we do it to get attention; sometimes we do it to dismiss a long-standing self-absorbing fault. For similar reasons we ridicule others.

Creative Humor

But often enough, humor is about human resourcefulness. Consider, for instance, the liturgy. The priest begins the liturgy, leads the penitential rite, and says the opening prayer. Then we hear the readings. Everything has been printed; everything has been read and recited for years and years. In the midst of this very familiar ritual, the priest has to get us into a space where we are willing to listen to something new. So what does he do? He tells a joke, a funny story, or an anecdote. He limbers us up from the routine and tries to stir in us a change. Something new is going to be said; that's his role as preacher, after all, to make the Word, the Good News. And so to break the routine, he uses humor to create space, to make us alert and to touch our humanity. It's fairly familiar and fairly effective. A friend of mine wrote, "A local priest began every homily with a joke and after awhile, we smiled beforehand when he rose to speak."

Humor achieves this same creative space when a family member makes a witty remark in order to lighten a tense situation. That remark takes the family to higher, yet closer ground. Humor allows us to distance ourselves from a situation and to get a different perspective.

Humor in the Face of Adversity

Humor helps us to deal with adversity. When I was at Fordham living in the dorms, the resident advisors (RAs) began the year with ice-breakers for the students in their particular corridors. Those silly games were all designed to expose everyone's humanity. Like the preacher who tells the joke, the orientation leader who starts with this-year's-newest-dumb-interaction-game is trying to get people to relax. Both are sympathetic with their congregations, trying to help them enjoy life precisely when they are taking it most seriously, whether at a liturgy or at the beginning of a school year. Humor helps us to face what we should, while reminding us of our humanity and our capacity for enjoyment.

It is why at times we get punchy. We get punchy as a reaction to tension. Tension rises, expectations are evident, seriousness is called for, and suddenly we start laughing like we're in the second-grade. Punchiness is our release from tension. Though punchiness isn't a virtue, it captures the essence of humor, that is, the way laughter reminds us of our humanity and of our capacity for enjoyment. Unfortunately unlike humor, punchiness does not help us face what we should. Punchiness just wants us to escape.

Humor is a practice we cultivate to make light hearted and bearable the situations in which we find ourselves. A good sermon will bring us close to something very central, a truth that we don't normally consider. To bring us closer the preacher doesn't tell a joke only to make us appreciate a shift in the liturgy or to understand our humanity, but also to make our approach to something so dreadfully important more easy. Humor helps us access the difficult.

And, if we remember a funny story, we can be sure that it was funny because it lightened us up. Think of the stories that we know as funny, stories that we tell within our families or among our circle of friends, stories that we repeat whenever we reunite. Why do we repeat them? Why are they part of a family's memorabilia? Why are they savored?

Probably because of the situation in which the original story occurred. Inevitably there was some tension, some sadness, some fear, or some anxiety. Perhaps it was about driving, taking an exam, attending an important meeting, or dealing with bad news. Funny stories usually occur when something problematic is on the horizon and suddenly someone does or says something – unexpectedly – and breaks the tension. Somehow they remind us of our humanity, our capacity for enjoyment and our surprise at the unpredictable.

Humor and Human Affection

Why is it that we repeat those stories? I think that we don't tell the stories to simply laugh, we tell them because we're trying to catch the affection we felt in that moment when we all were so surprised and laughed. That's why it is so hard to tell a funny story to someone else. The humor of the story is filled with the affection for the people involved in the story and with a perception of the threat that initially was there. If the listener knows the people in the story she can perhaps appreciate what the adversity meant to them and why it was funny that they reacted as they did. If not, she will say, "I guess I had to have been there."

Those family stories or those stories among friends are part of the legacies of our relationships. They can only be told successfully within related circles. Good humor is about each of us celebrating our vulnerability, and we usually only do that with those with whom we feel we can. Good humor depends on familiarity. Without the familiarity we lose the humor.

Not so tragedy. Tell a sad story, about anyone, even a stranger. People react; they are drawn into it. They are caught into the tragedy; they ask concerned questions. Questions about the details, the causes, the well-being of those involved. Tell a funny story and see how many questions you get asked.

Tragedy is about fate and the tragic story reminds us of how our humanity is ultimately out of our hands. When we hear a tragic story, we huddle with the victim. But humor rejects fate and limitations. It's not at all about being a victim; it's about being inventive, at our own cost. Humor is about human creativity in the face of difficulty. When it is staged it takes a master to make us laugh: Charlie Chaplin holding the hand of a clock, John Candy and Steve Martin missing a plane, or Lucille Ball trying to decorate cakes on a conveyor belt. When it is with those whom we love, we laugh easily and delightfully, celebrating even more our very vulnerable humanity.

✵

TWENTY-ONE

Physical Fitness

WHEN I WAS SEVEN YEARS OLD AND ATTENDING ST. THOMAS Aquinas Grammar School in Brooklyn, John F. Kennedy was elected president. I thought he was the greatest: smart, quick, funny, young, nice family. As president, he got only better. I had only one reservation: in the first year of his presidency, he insisted that the nation's youth become more physically fit. He demanded gym classes in our schools. I did not like him for that. I thought, physical fitness is for those who could; I couldn't. Schools were for brains, not bodies. Luckily at St. Thomas Aquinas, they were not convinced of his demands. Gym classes were not taken terribly seriously and my only humiliation was when they insisted on us doing somersaults. I could never do a somersault.

High school was another story. When I had to take "phys ed" courses each year, I thought often on President Kennedy. This was his fault. Sure he came from a family with broad shoulders and quick legs. Not me. As I faced parallel bars, I believed deeply that they were designed by some person whom I never knew but who wanted only to humiliate me. I hated the ropes. I burned my hands whenever I would start sliding down them; my only good fortune was that I never got that high. I especially thought that the rings were dangerous; I would tell the instructor that my mother's shoulder dislocated on occasion and I was afraid I inherited her genes. He didn't believe me. After the way I bounced around on those rings, I learned, beyond a doubt, that my shoulders would never dislocate.

At seventeen, I entered the Jesuit novitiate, I lost a lot of weight and I began running. By the time I went to study theology nine years later I could do a few sports. None well, but I wasn't terrified of them. I never played team sports; I was a loner: jogging, swimming, biking, and later weights. As one of my students said to me: we're divided into two classes, those who like teams, and those who do not. I'm in the second group. Now in my family with the exception of a brother-in-law and a nephew, I'm probably the most inclined to sports. This is comical.

Yet, I like doing some exercise. I feel great when and after I do them. I get hurt often enough: broken ankles from running in Rome; torn calf muscles from running in the Bronx; a bad shoulder from weights in Cambridge. But this is incidental.

A friend said to me, "Why are you calling physical fitness a virtue? It sounds awfully yuppie." (He writes about liberation theology.) I know he has a point, but I think that sports has something to do with our perceptions of our bodies. If we enjoy our bodies, we like sports; if we don't, we don't. I know that as a youngster I hated my body. I would have traded it in easily.

The Importance of the Human Body for Christians

Today I believe that our bodies are terribly important, not only because we are human, but more importantly, because we are Christians and, in particular, Catholics. This might seem strange, but consider this: among believers, Christians and Jews are the two most concerned with the body; among them, Catholics are the probably unsurpassed in their interests. As Christians, we believe that God *became* human flesh and dwelt among us. We acknowledge that we are made in God's image. We hope for the resurrection of the body (in fact, all the early conciliar formulas expressed belief in the resurrection of the body, not of the dead) and believe that our Lord appeared as risen in the flesh and reigns today. Our central act of worship concerns the real presence of Jesus Christ in the bread and wine which we proclaim is the body and blood of Christ and which we partake by eating and drinking them. And we call the Church, the People of God or the Body of Christ. Is that visceral enough? Our God, our self-understanding, our hope, our worship and our Church are each expressed in the language of body.

Catholicism, in particular, has elected the body as a primary mode of expression. Its emphasis on the sacramental accentuates this regard for the physical. Its language, art, and culture are extraordinarily corporeal. Think for a minute of the Sistine Chapel, a very Catholic place. I first saw it with a colleague who, after commenting on the ceiling and rear wall frescoes by Michelangelo, showed me the side wall panels by Raphael, Pinturicchio, Ghirlandaio and others who depicted scenes from the lives of either Moses and the old law or Jesus and the new law. As if to reiterate these frescoes' themes, each is entitled with a word derived from the Latin word for law, *lex*. My colleague remarked, "Here, this is where the cardinals sit and elect the pope. What goes on in their minds when the only word they see is "law" and the empty throne sitting at the base of Michelangelo's Last Judgment?"

I saw something else. I imagined the cardinals sitting there with great nude paintings. They elect the pope surrounded with images of the flesh, some attractive and some not. Sure there's law, but there is also the most concrete expression of humanity, the nude human body. In a way if the great wrestling match of modern thought is between the mind and the body, then the canvas for that match may well be the Sistine Chapel where law meets the nude body.

Taking the Body Seriously

In the Church's life the body has always been key. Aquinas, when he described the "order" of charity said that we ought to love God, ourselves, our neighbor and our bodies, in that order. He believed first that we ought to love God as the first commandment tells us and that both naturally and spiritually we should love ourselves next (not unlike the virtue of self-care above). Thomas meant by self-love that we should care for ourselves enough so as to be responsible for ourselves and for answering to the call of salvation. After self-love, we must love our neighbor, and after our neighbor, our bodies. Certainly we may think it strange for Thomas to distinguish self-love from love for our bodies. But that issue aside, Thomas wrote in the *Summa Theologiae* that concretely we ought literally to care for and love our bodies. But what did he concretely mean? For that answer we have to look at other writings. For instance, every Advent and Lent at the University of Paris there were enormous assemblies during which major professors took to the stage and people in the audience asked whatever question they wanted. In fact, these sessions were called the "whatevers" (Latin: *Quodlibetales*). Thomas regularly volunteered for these sessions: One "whatever" was "Is it ever permitted to take warm baths and stay in them for a moderate period of time"? Certainly, answered Thomas, it was a healthy, relaxing and physically enjoyable activity.

Another Dominican, Catherine of Sienna, took a very different view of human life, though still one that was concerned with the physical. Whenever she wrote, she signed everything "in the blood of Christ." In the last years of her life she fed mostly on the body of Christ. And her dying words were, "Blood! Blood!" She was calling for Christ. She did not hate her body; on the contrary, as

Caroline Bynum has taught us in her *Holy Feast and Holy Fast,* Catherine realized that through her body she could communicate with Christ.

The medieval era does not only give us the hefty Thomas in a hot tub or the emaciated Catherine at the altar, it also gives us the athlete Sebastian. By the time the renaissance came, Sebastian along with young David and Saint Catherine of Alexandria became athletic saints and heroes. One saw in their bodies the strength of their faith. One wonderful celebration of this is the cathedral of Milan where the entire exterior is covered with statues of saints in great physical form; their bodies conveying their spiritual greatness, their virtuousness. The Christian athlete became then a metaphor for the saint, an extension, of course, of Paul's own metaphor of running the race.

Christians were not the only ones who saw their bodies as vehicles for their spiritual excellence. The Greeks loved their bodies. The Greeks took the body so seriously that health itself was a virtue. Why? Because if virtue was the sign of moral strength and order, then the virtuous person's body had to be able to express that strength and order. The idea is not much different from the later Christians. Both saw integration as key. For one the work of virtue conveyed itself in the body; for the other, the grace of Christ did. In any event, before the Enlightenment, every major culture that reflected on virtue considered care of or perfecting the body, virtuous activity. Each saw that the virtuous person or the saint ought to be evidently seen as virtuous. In their bodies, they were virtuous.

We today are too disembodied. We think virtue is not about the body, but about the soul: charity, faith, justice, sympathy. But our forebearers knew that the work of virtue penetrated the entire fabric of a human being: the whole heart, the whole mind, the whole body, the whole soul. If it is not the whole person that we want to see being perfected in all of her relationships then we have missed the entire point of this book.

Virtue is about bringing about what can be. I had in my "husky" pre-adolescent body the possibility of doing a somersault. When I finally learned how to do one, it was in part, because I was learning not only how to tuck my head, but also that my body, like my heart and my brain were God's gifts to me. Like those dimensions of myself, my body too needed to be exercised. For by exercise, I would become virtuous. We learn that, whenever we exercise our souls, our hearts, our brains, or our bodies.

Questions for Reflection

1. Do you enjoy practicing hospitality? If not, what could you do to help yourself become more hospitable?

____

____

____

____

2. Describe someone wise in your life. Why did you pick that person?

____

____

____

____

3. How do you practice gratitude?

____

____

____

____

4. What exercises do you do for physical fitness?

____

____

____

____

5. Are sympathy and humor different sides of the same coin?

____

____

____

____

6. Name three other virtues that you think merit reflection.

____

____

____

____